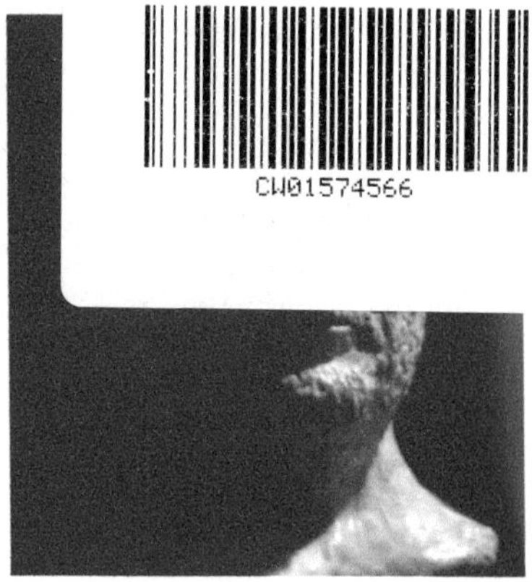

Jonathan 'Bill' Bayley is a retired science teacher, 75 next birthday, who lives in Warwickshire, with his wife of 51 years, and his two dogs. He has four granddaughters and three offspring scattered world-wide. The Town he lives in is a strong community, and he enjoys being a part of it. Although he only arrived in 1967, he is almost considered to be a native. He paints, and has had ten exhibitions locally. He is the editor of a writer's magazine, the Bear Flag, which has been going for over 10 years. His hobbies are pipe-smoking, psychology and thinking, amongst others. His previous book, "It's Not Working" was about the effect work has on one man's life. It is available at The DVD Shop, High St., Alcester, Warks, B49.

RUN A YOUTH CLUB IN TEN EASY STEPS

BY

JONATHAN 'BILL' BAYLEY

BEAR FLAG PUBLICATIONS

PUBLISHED BY : BEAR FLAG PUBLICATIONS.

ISBN 978-0-9569937-0-0

Printed in Great Britain by
the MPG Books Group, Bodmin and King's Lynn

I would like to dedicate this book to all those people who have helped me run youth clubs in my town, without whose help and sense of humour this would have been impossible; also to all the young people in those clubs, without whose presence and fascinating ways of going on this book would not exist.

RUN A YOUTH CLUB IN TEN EASY STEPS

STEP ONE -- GETTING THE IDEA.

Youth Clubs have a lot in common with Abattoirs. They perform similar functions. They process unruly materials so that they can be assimilated into the human race. Also, they generate a huge amount of waste matter that is simply thrown away. Yet very few people want to go to either, necessary though they may be. Everyone knows they exist, indeed they must exist, but not anywhere near human habitation, thank you. Almost like sewage farms, they keep disease harmlessly out of the way whilst performing a disinfecting function. Youth Clubs resemble lepers in the Middle Ages, best kept away from normal people lest they infect them with some dread disease. They should be founded deep in the countryside, although if they were, no youths would ever go. What would the youths do? Who cares?

A Youth Club is not a building, not a place. It is an idea, a concept that everyone understands. A Youth Club exists in a place all right, but not for long. It moves about, like the Wandering Jew. It is a tramp, or a gypsy, everyone knows what it is, but nobody welcomes it. Nobody wants it on their doorstep, not for long. Yet many think it is a Good Idea, there should be Youth Clubs, but not near them. They bring trouble. Worthy people run them, muscular Christians full of good intentions, or boxers who can bring discipline to the rowdy youths who come under their sway. Men with strong principles and the ability to communicate with lawless lunatics are the kind that run them. Reformed criminals are suitable candidates too, although the public wonder if the criminals are really reformed, and won't infect their charges with whatever miasma that sent them off the rails in the first place.

The public always think there should be a Youth Club somewhere, it's to keep the troublesome lads off the streets, but Not In My Back Yard, thanks very much. And they never do keep the lads off the streets. For one thing, they are only open a few hours a week, and the lads can be on the streets twenty-four hours a day. For another, the lads probably meet other lads there, and plot and plan their mayhem in the comfort of the Youth Club. But Clubs are seen as potentially Good, even though the practice of them creates a lot of trouble. But like most Christian principles, like "Love Thy Neighbour" and "Thou Shalt Not Kill". the moral bits are more honoured in the breach than the observance. God wants them to exist, even though the Devil rules there. Oh well, it can't be helped. That's how the world runs.

The History of Youth Clubs is a short one. There were none at all for millennia, then around 150 years ago, the first ones started. They were an invention of the Victorians, who saw lots of idle youth on the streets, unable or unwilling to get jobs, so they started educating them, and preaching Christianity to them. Then along came the YMCA, and then the Scouts. Neither would be though of as Youth Clubs today. The first statutory ones were in the late Fifties, when there was a public panic about the barbaric Youth Culture. They provided shelter, activities and adults to be bounced off, all very suitable for disaffected young people. No-one had much idea of what was their purpose, since Christianity and boxing were definitely out of favour. So what else was there? Just milling about with your mates was the commonest activity, but this didn't satisfy the Do-gooders, or the funders. So they had a kind of limbo life, rising and falling with the tides of human fashion and inclination. It is not clear whether the kids would have run them themselves if they had been allowed to hire premises, but they were not, so that never arose. Probably they would not have run them, as all the kids wanted was a kind of junior pub. Some places actually ran clubs like that in pubs, without alcohol, of course, but not for long. They went the way of all youth clubs, here today and gone tomorrow.

Of course, this book will no more tell you how to run a youth club than the Bible tells you how to be good, or an art book tells you how to paint. It cannot be done in a book. You simply have to do it. Try it out, find where the difficulties are, then go to the book for guidance. This book will give you no guidance either. That is because each youth club is unhappy in its own way. No, it was Tolstoy said that about families. But it applies to youth clubs too. Like families, they can also be happy. Just not for very long.

So what does this book do then? It will try to tell you about one man's experience with youth clubs, in one small town in the middle of England. He has no idea how typical his experience is, since he knows no other youth clubs, but he has been involved for nearly thirty-five years in this one. That should be enough for some kind of picture to become apparent, even if it may be fuzzy and imprecise. It is colourful, even vivid, although the colours may be bizarre and harsh at times. They will not match the colour scheme of your lounge, certainly. They will not match anything, except the jarring tones of teenage dress.

The Town is Elcaster, in South Warwickshire. Nobody

famous ever came from there, although the world's best playwright and poet was allegedly born and raised in an adjacent town in Tudor times. He may even have been born in Elcaster instead of The Other Town-on-Avon, but so far no evidence has been found. We in Elcaster have not given up, though, and research is continuing to prove that this is the Town that should have the Birthplace, and the RSC, and all the other things that make The Other Town so famous, where Elcaster is not. Fame has got a double edge, though. It does not always bring Fortune. Just walk the streets of Stratford (for that is the name of The Other Town) to see the thousand ways that tourists can be fleeced, duped and patronised. Elcaster has no tawdry tourist shops because it has no tourists. It has pride, though. It was a Town in Roman times, when Stratford was a collection of muddy huts beside the Avon ford, on the road to London from the salt deposits of Droitwich, from Wales and even Ireland.

I came to live in this town in the late Sixties. I brought my wife and three small children to a semi-detached house on a new estate on the edge of the town. I had got a teaching job in Birmingham, twenty miles away, and thought that Elcaster looked a good place to bring up my children and to belong to a community that I could fit into without much effort. I was right about the first, my kids loved it. The second was not so easy. All communities require an effort to get into, and Elcaster was harder than most, at least at first.

My wife and I had lived in or near small market towns

most of our lives, except when we went to college in the Fifties, in London. Both of us had loved being students there, but it was no place to live when married with children. I had worked in Swindon for a few years before moving up to Elcaster. We had three small kids. We bought a semi on an estate, and moved up between Christmas and New Year in 1967.

It was horrible. It rained on the day we moved, the kids were grouchy, the new house felt like an unheatable shed, the only people we could talk to were the ones living next door, and they were weird, with no kids of their own. The road was black ash and thick mud. We tried to make things cosy, but our hearts were not in it. Everyone wanted to go home. Especially me. All this was My Fault. I had to get another job, now we were at the end of the universe, with no way back. I knew I had made a wrong decision. My wife knew something too, but it wasn't that. It was "Push on". Bless her.

Things were no better in the morning. New Year's Eve. Despondent beyond belief, I tried not getting up, but my wife would have none of that. I took them all for a "little drive round the Town". This depressed us all much further. What did we expect on New Year's Eve, for God's sake? We came "home" and ate hot buttered toast, Suddenly, things brightened up. We ate our presents, played some games, it was bedtime soon. They went up with hardly a murmur. I went to look at them all sleeping later. What had I brought them to? It couldn't be all bad, they looked so peaceful and warm and safe. I felt the same, for the first time.

STORY OF A BOY

The water was black as ink as the ship nosed its way past clumps of reeds towards the faint firelight on the far bank. The figure at the helm was wrapped against the bitter cold, and the boy stood at the prow, ready to jump off and tie the ship up at the bank. The pilot, a large man dressed in animal skins, pointed to the fire. The helmsman guided the craft to a gentle stop, the boy leaped off and secured the rope to a stump. The darkness was complete. There were faint sounds of water.

"Is this it, Joseph?", asked the boy. The man nodded as he stepped ashore, and stretched, glad to be free again from steering his precious ship.

"Yes, this is where the feast is to be held. Let's see now, where's the Chief?" A group of fierce men loomed out of the dark, speaking in a strange guttural tongue. One gripped Joseph's hand in his, and beckoned them both to follow him. He spoke to Joseph as they walked.

"What's he say, Joseph?", said the boy.

"He says that they saw the sun move a hair's breadth towards the East this morning at sunrise, so that they know this is the day for the Feast. They say the earth is not dying, the days will get longer again, and summer will come. It is their Yule, the Feast of Rebirth. We are privileged to be invited. It must be the gold that we brought that makes us important to them. And the tin that we carry back."

"What will the Feast be like, Joseph? Will it be like we have in the Temple?"

"No, lad. We are far from home. You are only eleven, but you have seen many sights that even adults in our land have never seen. You are lucky."

They trudged on through the thick darkness, flurries of snow brushing against their cheeks from time to time. The boy piped up again.

"Where exactly are we, Joseph? It's Britain, but what's this place called?"

"We are on the Isle of Avalon, my boy. It's a sacred place, surrounded by swamps and difficult to find. That's why we had a guide. Hardly any foreigners have ever been allowed to come here, certainly not at the Yuletide Feast."

They reached a village. In the centre was a large hut, and they went in. The air was thick with smoke. Food of all kinds was piled up at the sides of the hut, but the boy's eye was taken by a huge log near the fire. Their guides bade them sit, and then the feast began.

They had many dishes they had never eaten before, delicate meats, grilled fish, breads, spiced grains, soups, stews, and finally a sweet cake. They drank thin beer, sweet mead, and a little wine. They felt full. Then the ceremony began.

It seemed to focus on the colossal log at first. A small log was brought in already alight, and the big log was placed on it, and the flames fanned until they roared. There was singing and dancing, all highly disciplined. Then the chief struck the log, and a cheer went up as tens of thousands of sparks shot upwards to disappear into the darkness above. Joseph whispered to the boy. "They believe that God will grant them a cow for each spark. They worship a different God to us."

"Perhaps not," said the boy, "For in my Father's house are many mansions."

Joseph looked puzzled, The boy was always coming out with strange sayings. Where did he get them from? He was an odd one, this lad.

The boy leaned over and whispered to Joseph. "Joseph, perhaps I shall have my birthday on this day. The day the whole Earth is reborn. I can see that may come to pass, though I know not how it may be so."

Joseph frowned. "Come on, young Jesus, time we were on our way."

At this stage, I had no idea at all about running a youth club. I had never even been to one. I hardly knew of their existence. My youth up until the age of 14 was spent in a middle-class ghetto, Gerrards Cross, in Buckinghamshire. Our house was in a lovely setting, bang in the middle of Dukes Wood. The road we lived on was Dukes Wood Drive, and it wasn't even made up. It had lots of stones in it, that later would be most useful for our weapon of choice, the elastic-powered catapult. I was about seven when we went to live there, and at once it seemed like Heaven. The woods in front of us went on and on for ever, we never really got to the farthest boundaries. There were lakes there, and abandoned fields, and the woods were proper English oak, beech, ash and a few others. No dark firs at all. Ripe for birds nests, rabbits, and snakes. Adders. We were very scared of them, but they slid away fast when they heard us coming. Nobody but we boys ever seemed to go in them, although occasionally we would meet tractors and woodsmen, who cut a few trees down and stacked the logs into long cords, perfect for our forts. But the trees hardly seemed to diminish in number. In the harsh winter of 1947, we used to drag logs home and our Dad would cut them up. We had fires in the woods, and battles, everything a boy's heart could wish for.

For my seventh birthday I was give a dog, a terrier bitch we called Mary. Her brother lived next door, and was called George, so we thought it right to name our dog after the Royal Family. She was a great little dog, with an uncut tail that curled over like a pig's. She loved balloons and fireworks, picking up bangers and shaking them even when they exploded in her mouth. I could never work out how she could do that unharmed. She had two puppies, one all black and one black and white. My best friend Pete had the black one, and he called him Kim. I kept the other, naming him Mr. Porkins after an A.A. Milne story. I liked the name, but he got called Porky, and people thought it was because of his pig's tail, but he and I knew different.

From that time onwards Pete and I would spend all our time with the three dogs in the woods. The dogs loved it, searching for rabbits constantly. They only ever caught one, a dopey teenager they surprised in a bramble bush, but they never forgot their triumph. We took our catapults with us, shooting at trees, birds (never hitting one). We had bows and arrows too, home-made from hazel branches and string. We had crab-apple slingers as well, a long piece of hazel which when you impaled an apple on one end, and slung it fast, the apples could go over tall trees. They hurt if they hit you, too.

Later on, we had air-guns. These came on the scene just as we were getting stuck into some serious battles with local lads. Mostly they were from middle-class homes further up the road, they were just different gangs, but occasionally we met the yobs, who went to the local school. We were scared of them, and they were equally scared of us, because we outnumbered them, so they didn't often engage in pitched fights. But when they did, it was no holds barred. Catapults, bows and arrows, air-guns, we fought behind the piles of logs. How nobody got seriously hurt I do not know, but they didn't.

I got into serious trouble over my air-gun,though. We used to fight guerrilla battles in the back gardens, moving silently in groups to outwit each other. I was in my own garden one day, with my .177 rifle loaded and up to my shoulder, ready to fire. I sensed someone was behind next-door's shed, and sure enough, out came one of the Miller twins, detested enemies of ours, snobbish and gutless. As he moved out slowly, he clearly had not seen me. I had his fat chin in my sights. My gun was very accurate, there was no risk I would hit his eye. I knew it was wrong, I knew it. But I pulled the trigger.

Nothing ever in my life has compared with the elation I felt as he yelped, and ran away. I knew I had hit his massive chin. I also knew trouble was coming down the road. And so it did. Mr. Miller was irate and loud, dragging his sorry-looking son behind him with a big red mark right in the middle of his chin. My Dad had no choice, I knew that. I was in the wrong. So my air-gun was put away for a whole year. But I still think it was worth that spurt of joy I felt as I shot him. It was such a perfect chance, perfectly executed. Nobody died. I'm still proud of it. But I didn't tell my son so. Lord of the Flies contains a considerable truth about boys.

What I did at home was always fun, and I did a lot. Balsa wood models were popular, and I made lots, including gliders, elastic-powered flyers. I had a Hornby DoubleO train set, on a big board in my bedroom. I made puppets, I collected stamps, I bought conjuring tricks to perform for my parents, until they went wrong and I burst into tears and ran to my bedroom, leaving my family helpless with laughter. I had chemistry sets, grew crystals, read my parents' books. And I read a lot. Agatha Christie, A.A. Milne, Sherlock Holmes, Father Brown, Ngaio Marsh, Tales of Detection, Mystery and Horror, Rudyard Kipling, Rider Haggard, John Buchan, Edgar Wallace, H.G.. Wells science fiction, Olaf Stapleton, Contraception for Adults (incomprehensible rubbish), and hundreds more. I read the papers too, and listened to the radio. Children's Hour, In Town Tonight, Music Hall, Workers Playtime, Dick Barton, The Man in Black. My grandmother sent me Chick's Own and the Children's Newspaper, both of which I had to hide from my friends in shame. I never read either, but she did send me Rainbow, which wasn't bad.

My problem was not at home. It was at my Prep School, Thorpe House. The name still sends a shudder through my soul. I just hated it. And they hated me.

I never found out why my parents chose that particular school. Clearly the local school was quite out of the question, because my parents' kind did not send their children there. It had to be fee-paying, and there were a few Prep. Schools around. I think they chose Thorpe House because it had a better reputation for sports that the others. Certainly my parents made no effort to find out what kind of education I was to get, they just sent me to the schools that their friends used, and assumed that was all there was to education. In those days, that was pretty much right.

I went there in 1944, a year before the War ended. I could read and write, having learned those from a Kindergarten. I suppose I looked forward to going to a New School. I was soon to be disappointed. If you have ever read George Orwell's account of his prep. school, St. Cyprian's, 'Such, such were the joys', you can get a faint whiff of what Thorpe House was like in 1944, about 25 years after Orwell's foul experiences.

You got the aura of the place the minute you stepped into the Hallowed Halls. Stale cabbage, chalk dust, dried school ink, farts, and damp. It was not an atmosphere in which young minds could grow and flourish; any mind coming into contact with that toxic air would immediately shrivel and perish. The school had a main building which was a large house, in which the Headmaster and his wife lived, and a few functions were performed, like cooking the execrable school meals and teaching seven-year-olds. The rest was made up of wooden huts, cold and badly lit. Outside was a 'playground', solid earth (mud in wet weather), tufts of dead grass, and a small patch of concrete. The games fields were a couple of miles away, where we walked every Wednesday in a crocodile, and back again. There was not a tree, no flowers, no green grass, nor any natural living item within yards of the place, as if the miasma it exhaled killed all forms of life stone dead.

The subjects taught were minimal. They were chosen to fit the Common Entrance for the Public Schools. They were

Arithmetic, English, Geography, History, French, Latin, Music and Religious Knowledge. There was no PE, no Art, nothing creative of any kind, not a trace of science. Games were once a week, Wednesday afternoon, with no changing rooms, no showers, no washing facilities of any kind, nor any toilets at the games field.

If the syllabus was dull, the staff were even duller. It was 1944, and any man of substance had gone to fight, so all we were left with were the rejects, the vicious elderly ladies, the men too old to be of use, and the Headmaster, Mr. Maurice. Why he was not called up remains a mystery, but we never questioned it. The school was owned by his father, Old Mr. Averill, who had Disseminated Sclerosis, and was a quivering lump of flesh in the corner of the Head's study, a rug round his useless legs. He could barely speak, but was an object of intense fear for all the boys, who regarded him as a deformed malignant monster, and he never gave any evidence to counter this. He was never wheeled out for any event, and we all believed that he passed his entire time in his feral corner, sleeping, defecating and eating there like a dying beast in a zoo. I met with him/it several times, but more of that later.

Right from the start, the school had nothing I wanted. Except other boys. I got on all right with most of them, made a lot of friends and enjoyed the break-times. We played the usual games, marbles, conkers, 'He' of all kinds, catch. We read the comics we bought on the way to school, Wizard,

Rover, Hotspur, all solid text from front to back, we read each one in less than a day, and swapped round so we read them all. We also read the Dandy and the Beano, but they were mostly cartoons and were quick to get finished. I drank in the politics from my parents' table, and became the only Socialist in the school, except for my friend Hughes, who chickened out around election time anyway, so he was no help. I learned to argue with my back to the wall, surrounded by older boys, rabid Tories, supporters of Good Old Winston Churchill, whom I said was a warmonger and deserved to lose the 1945 election to Attlee. I learned the hard way to make my audience laugh, just a little, so they wouldn't hit you when the real opponents looked like losing. You got listeners a tiny bit on your side if you made them laugh, and that tiny bit was enough to protect your hide. I never converted anyone to my cause, but I never changed my mind. I still haven't, Although all the Socialists like Nye Bevan, Clem Attlee, Ernie Bevan, are all gone, and all we have now is closet Tories like Blair and Mandelson, I still believe in the principles of socialism, not so far from the Christianity of Jesus.

After break, it was back to the classroom. I really learned almost nothing there, except in Maths, taken by Mr. Maurice. He was simplistic and brutal in his methods, caning you if you failed a test. I never did, because I liked maths, but not because of the way he taught it. I just found it intriguing, the way geometry could be proved, QED, the way Algebra solved puzzles with letters instead of numbers, and even arithmetic was useful, if dull. How many ditches got dug in how many days, baths filled with several taps, all ridiculous, but at least I could do them. Mr. Maurice must have been as thick as a brick, because one day he admitted that logarithms was as far as he had ever got in Maths, and that with a lot of difficulty. Even I could see there was a lot of maths beyond them, and he couldn't understand it? Thicko.

There was one other teacher worthy of the name, Mr. Beloe, who taught Latin and RE. He was very old, at least 50, and ate a lot of Melloids, tiny black throat sweets, all the time. It was years before I realised why. He was a drinker, his nose sported the most enormous grog-blossom, and he ate Melloids to hide the smell of drink. Even just after breakfast he smelled of Melloids. He must have polished off a lot of grog. But he had an idea of how to catch boys' attention. R.E. consisted of reading the Old Testament, and going through the stories there. David and Absalom, Goliath, Samson and Delilah, Moses, Baal, Jonah and the Whale, David and Jonathan, Saul. I can remember a lot about those stories, and old Beloe made them live somehow. He had no religion at all, I should imagine, and we never touched the New Testament, but the OT is full of great stories of war, death, destruction, adultery, heroism, enough to feed the interests of a class of boys in the late 40s, used to all those things.

We could sometimes distract him into recounting his

WWI experiences. These I realise now he must have made up, since no war veteran I have ever met wanted to recount his stories of the trenches. But old Beloe did, and they were better than the OT, sometimes. Sometimes not, though. He was not nearly so good as a Latin teacher. He didn't know much about the Romans, so we had to learn from the Eating Primer, as Kennedy was called, and massively dull it was too. I could never remember the declensions, conjugations, cases, tenses and other rubbish, it meant nothing to me. We translated into English, back into dead Latin. Dreary, dead and dull beyond measure.

The other teachers were barely even human. None of them lasted long anyway. English was endless parsing of sentences, never any writing of stories. Essays, 'A Day in the Life of a Penny', 'What I did on my Holidays', 'How to mend a puncture', my God, what a bore! I learned all my English at home by reading books. The only book I recall reading round the class was 'Jane Eyre'. Jane Eyre! In a class of eleven-year-old boys! What idiot thought that up? Mr. Jones, a raw-boned Irishman, that's who. Presumably not eligible for call-up because he was Irish, he knew next to no English, and could not teach to save his life.

One of the worst was 'Smudger' Smith. He was paid to teach French. He never taught anyone a single thing in his life. He must have been a mental case, because as soon as he started to speak, someone would make a silly noise,or shout, just do anything. He then became a gibbering wreck, unable to speak, but stamp up and down in his black gown, shouting, "Um...Um..." We ignored him, and got on with reading, talking, peashooter fighting, or whatever took our fancy. Once, a jackdaw owned by a boy called Dawes came looking for his owner, and perched on the open windowsill. Smudger started his usual rant, whereupon the bird panicked and flew into the room. It flapped blackly around, with Smudger flapping equally blackly beneath him, shouting his mantra, "Um...Um...". The bird answered all our prayers, and settled on his bald head, making him wave his arms like a demented dervish. The jackdaw then crapped all down Smudger's neck, and flew out of the window. We were all helpless on the floor by now, unable to speak, but storing up that treasured scene in our minds, to be replayed again and again, to our children and grandchildren. Better than video!

At times, Mr. Maurice would pass by outside, when Smudger would miraculously calm down until he had gone by, then resume his imbecilic rant when it was safe. The rumour was that he had been damaged by a bomb blast, but he should not have been teaching. I don't suppose he charged Thorpe House much money, though. What sort of life did he have outside the school, I wonder? We never thought of things like that then.

I was very often in trouble. I was bored out of my mind. I had a very low boredom threshold then, and still do. I got careless, and was caught performing some wicked deed to amuse my friends, or at least myself. The form punishment took was a strange one, and grossly unfair, or so I thought. Good deeds were rewarded by a Star, on a pink slip like a bank cheque. But teachers only ever awarded 'quarter-stars', so you had to keep this grotty little pink piece of tatty paper, and produce it next time a teacher rewarded you. When all four quarters were filled in, you gave them in, and they were recorded on a chart, House by House. (The Houses were Tudor, Lancaster, York and another, I forget what. I think it was Windsor. How imaginative! I was in Tudor, House colour... Pink. Ugh!) The punishments were doled out differently. They were called Stripes, and you always got a whole one, written out on a pale blue piece of trashy paper. These were to be handed in to the Headmaster first thing in the morning.

It was no use losing the Stripe and hoping no-one would notice. The Stripe had a counterfoil, just like a cheque, and the Head looked at teachers' Stripe books regularly. If you were discovered to have had a Stripe and had not handed it in, you got double the number of strokes of the cane. The performance of Handing in a Stripe is worth recording for its sadism and cruelty.

You knocked at the Head's door, Stripe in hand. Mr. Maurice opened the door, you went in, and there in the corner was The Horror, Old Mr. Averill, like a huge and evil toad, full of venom. Mr. Maurice would take your Stripe, hand it to the Horror, who took an age to pretend to read it, his brown-spotted flabby hand shaking violently while he did so. His drool-covered jowls shook even more. (I am not exaggerating. I used to be terrified of this monster). His drooping eyes rose to stare at you, red-rimmed and watering, and he slowly slobbered out the same words every time. "Beat him, Maurice!" The worst was over then. The beating hurt like hell, but it was not terrifying. The only words I ever heard that frightful old man utter were those, "Beat him, Maurice." I must have heard them over a dozen times. He never asked me anything, never appeared human in any way. I was 8 when this happened to me first, and he haunted my dreams from then on. He no longer does, because he is dead. I would wish him in Hell, but I don't believe in it. Besides, he must have been in Hell then, poor old bastard. Serve him right, though. I think he ruled his son Maurice like a tyrant, since he had the qualifications ('Cantab.' on the brass plate by the front door), and poor old dim Maurice had none, except a Certificate in Maths, which was not good enough to run a prep school, or a p*ss-up in a brewery. Still, Maurice made up for it in real nastiness, for which you don't get certificates. Maurice would have got a Doctorate Summa Cum Laude.

I travelled to school by bus at first, often arriving late. This didn't matter, as you missed Assembly, with its dreary hymn and empty prayers. Latecomers were let in to the back of the stage to hear the day's notices. I think it was supposed to be humiliating, but I never paid any heed, since nobody else did. To catch the bus, I had to walk up our road, through a stretch of woodland, onto the Windsor Road. I used to cry all through that wood, knowing nobody could see me, and I would dry my eyes only when I got to the bus-stop. I think I did that for at least four years. I really hated going to Thorpe House, although my friends were all there, and I never cried when I got there. It was just not done.

I did all I could to avoid going to school. I learned to fake illness with consummate skill, fooling my mother often. I would listen to the radio, Housewives Choice, Music While You Work, then the schools' programmes, which were very good. Then Worker's Playtime, the News, the Afternoon Play, Mrs. Dale's Diary, and if I picked the right time, the commentary of the TT Races from the Isle of Man. The sound of the British motorbikes, BSAs, Nortons, Matchless, coming down Craig-ny-Baa was magic to my ears. I could sometimes fake days on end, but eventually my mother would send me back to Hell. Why she never asked what was wrong with school I never knew. I was known to be a Problem Child, so it was All My Fault anyway. That is how things were in those days. Schools were supposed to be dull. It's how you learned about Life.

A few events stand out in my memory like vivid scars. The Alleged Bullying of Howe was one. I used to cycle to school after a while, as I had a new bike, a solid steel black monster, where my friends all had the new aluminium ones. I was walking it out of the school with my friend Peter Bridges, the son of a chemist in the High Street, a lad who wouldn't say boo to a goose. As we walked and chatted over the day's events, this little twerp named Howe followed us, and called us names. Since he was at least two years younger, we ignored him. He went on and on, so by the time we got to the railway embankment, we enticed him over, and menaced him, just to shut him up. I told him that if he went on, we would roll him down the bank into the path of the express to London, and he would be cut up into such small pieces that his own granny would not recognise him. He went away, suitably cowed, and we continued our walk.

Next morning, there was hell to pay. Mr. Maurice had me in his study and told me I had bullied young Howe, my friend Peter Bridges had confessed, and I was to be punished in front of the whole school. Peter was let off for admitting his guilt. I said nothing, nor was my version of events asked for. I was paraded in front of the assembled pupils, my ghastly sin of bullying and intimidation of an innocent youngster were enumerated. It was said I had denied it (untrue, I had said nothing), and I was caned six of the best. I recall thinking as I bent over 'This is a fine way to deal with alleged bullying, a grown man whacking a boy of ten with a stick.' I was then made to give out the exam papers, another course in my humiliation put up by Mr. Maurice. I was supposed to feel sorry. I didn't. I felt nothing except impotent rage. Rage at the injustice of not being heard, rage at the injustice of the lies that Howe and his father must have told, rage at the way Mr. Maurice accepted their version without question.

This event did more to politicise me than anything in my whole life, before or since. Authority acting out its prejudices without anyone being able to question it has always made me angry. Whenever I was teaching and tempted to condemn a pupil before hearing his side of the question, I recalled this incident, and the impact it made on me. I didn't blame my mate Peter Bridges, he had been intimidated by Mr. Maurice, who just knew I was a bully, and saw a way to try and humiliate me. He failed, being a bully himself. It was only a lot later that I found out the reason Maurice Averill detested me so much.

Mr. Maurice only did one thing well in his whole life. He played Rugby for Wasps. He and his Rugby pals used to drink in a pub in Fulmer, The Black Horse, on a Saturday night, which was also where my parents drank, along with the hockey players from my Dad's team. My Dad was an intellectual Socialist, and he detested Rugby players, especially ones that thought a lot of themselves like Mr. Maurice and his chums. So there were arguments; my Dad was good at arguing, and used to humiliate his opponents with his knowledge and debating skills. Mr. Maurice had the debating skills of a numbskull parrot, and doubtless my Dad regularly humiliated him. So Maurice Averill, brave chap that he was, would take it out on me at school. QED.

That's enough about my dreadful school. I think it was not so dreadful to the other boys, as they expected to be bored, but I did not respond at all well to boredom. The only way to get on in Thorpe House was to be good at Sports, but I was not good enough. I did make the cricket team in my last year, and topped the bowling averages as a spinner, but Mr. Maurice didn't really rate cricket, it was not Manly enough (he was useless at it himself), and it was too intellectual for his anthropoid tastes. Mr. Prodger was the Cricket expert. I could write a book about Mr. Prodger, straight out of Beachcomber via the Saloon bar of the local pub. Mr. Prodger was an ass, a leaden, dim-witted, pompous ex-used-car salesman with a loud mouth unconnected to his sluggish brain cell. He taught us Science as well as Geography in my last year there, yet he knew nothing whatsoever about the subject, save what he dimly remembered from his own school days. He made hydrogen by mixing sodium metal and water, which is very dangerous indeed, and how he never blew himself and us to Kingdom Come I shall never know. But Mr. Prodger was typical of the kind of 'teacher' you got in the late 40s in bad private schools -- unemployable anywhere, a man amongst boys, a fool to all grown men. There are still plenty of them around, running British Industry into the ground.

I did try to find some way to contact the other ordinary lads of Gerrards Cross, by joining the local Scout troop. I got on all right with them, though none of my prep school friends joined with me. They taught me to scrump apples , how to shoplift without being caught, and various other ways of going on that they thought were essential for survival. I cannot recall them ever teasing me about my private school, as they all went to the local one. I did go to a Scout Camp in Wales for a week, but I was so homesick, I cried all the time. There was no going home, it was too far for parents to fetch you, so I had to sob and bear it. It was good for me, in a weird way. I cannot remember why I left the Scouts, I suspect my parents found they were not a Good Influence on me, and sent me as a boarder at Thorpe House for my last year there. I was furious. Betrayed my my own parents, into the hands of that bloody bully! Bored all the time now, not just during the school day, I must have worked, because I got a scholarship to my minor public school, Clayesmore. Only one teacher at Thorpe House ever told me I was clever. That was the French teacher, M. Jammes, who asked me one day why I fooled about so much, as with a little effort I could pass this simple exam. I was amazed. No-one had ever said that to me before, except my mother, and mothers always said that kind of lie to their sons. My one regret about getting that scholarship is that Mr. Maurice could put my name up in gold letters on his Scholarship Board, to show off to prospective parents. He had nothing to do with it, and I wished I could break in to the school and scratch it out.

I found myself in Paradise at my new Public school. For I was classed as intelligent there, because I had got a scholarship. Right from the start I responded to their expectations. I had not realised how depressed I must have been at Thorpe House, because they classed me as a troublemaker. Thorpe House expected nothing from me, and I gave them what they deserved, nothing. I did make trouble

-- because I was bored stiff by their petty rules, their dreary teachers, their 'sporting' ethic, and their unjust way of treating me. So I lived up to their way of seeing me, I knew nothing better. Looking back, I feel I was like those dogs that psychologists put in situations that are impossible to escape from, situations that the dog hates and is getting punished repeatedly, yet cannot find a way to do the right thing and get a reward. These cruel experiments would not be allowed now, but reading about them made me think, I was like those dogs. The result is that the dog just gives up, lies down and ceases to respond to any stimulus. In other words, it has induced depression. It is cured by treating the dog with rewards for responding to stimuli, and slowly it will shed its lethargic state and behave like a normal dog. It will slink away when shown the cage in which this occurred, for it remembers the dreadful experience. I would not slink away from Thorpe House now, I would shout as I went in, damning the whole lot to eternal fire for the way they treated me. But the place would be empty of anyone who was responsible. They must all be dead by now. Let us hope so, anyway.

STEP TWO --- INTRODUCTION.

STORY OF A BOY, 2.

The boy woke up in the dark. The air was very chill and damp, and he was shivering with the cold. His rough woollen blanket smelled of animals, and he knew he was not going to get back to sleep. He listened to the night sounds as they came through the clear cold air. They were all strange to him, quite unlike the comfortable noises of his warmer home. He couldn't recognise any at first, then he heard a cockerel crow, and the wind rustle the bare branches of the bushes around the hut that he was lying in. He heard the soft breathing of his master Joseph beside him, and the stirrings of the sheep around the outside of the hut.

He had come a long way, over the sea in the small boat with Joseph. Just the two of them, to meet some of the metal traders in this odd land, so cold and dark in the deep winter . He had wanted to come, his parents had given their blessing, it was an adventure. He knew his master was a kindly man, so he would be well treated. He had been very sick at first, especially when they rounded the huge rock and set out northwards into the vast ocean. It had seemed an age before they saw land, and the waves had appeared to engulf them, but Joseph told him to have no fear, God would protect them, and He had.

Oh, it was so cold! He knew he could lie there no longer, he had to get up and move around just to get warm. He crept out of the bed he lay in, quietly so as not to wake Joseph; he put on his thick woollen coat and his sandals, then put his head outside. The sharp cold air bit into his nostrils, and made him gasp. He stepped through the sheep and past the bushes. How strange that they had no leaves! Joseph said that many trees in this cold land shed their leaves in winter, it helped them to survive the bitter cold. He walked into an open space and gazed around.

The moon was full and glaring bright. The whole landscape was lit in a white light with black shadows, huge trees in clumps, a forest dark in the distance. The fields were bright with frost, they dazzled the boy, and he shaded his eyes as he watched for tiny movements amongst the shadows that might mean danger. Wolves he knew were common, and some bears had been seen nearby. He soon forgot them, transfixed as he was by the loveliness of what he saw. The light shone like silver on the river and the pools of water that stretched to the horizon, merging with the sea in the far distance. They had sailed here through those pools, full of fish and birds of all kinds. A heron screeched, and the boy jumped. An owl screamed, another hooted. The boy shivered, and started to walk.

He moved towards the Tor, the cone-like hill that the local priests held sacred. He could just make out the wooden structure at the top, some kind of altar to their strange Gods. He felt drawn towards the Tor, looming there in black shadow touched with silver. The great yew trees around the foot were black and silent as he moved under them towards the great spiral path that led to the summit. He smelled wood smoke, and heard snoring from the old druids that guarded the Tor, yet he felt no fear of them. He had met some, and liked their air of wisdom as they questioned him in his own tongue. They shook their heads over his answers, though. He panted as he climbed, and stopped to see the silent land laid out before him, so full of glory in white samite and ebony under the moon. It was his Father's land, strange and beautiful as anything he had ever seen, and he blessed it under his breath.

He was at the top. The sky was dark blue, and he watched a lighter layer appear in the East. The dawn would soon be here. The stars dimmed a little, as if in honour of the arrival of their King the Sun. The boy sat down and waited for the sunrise, and gave thanks to God for another day in such a lovely land. As the sun rose and shone its sudden warmth upon him, he stood and stretched out his arms to his side, glorying in the power of all his senses; the warmth of the sun, the blaze of its light, the cry of the birds, the scent of the frosty smoke, the taste of the icy air. He felt elated, like a King himself. He became the World, it was him and he was it, they were at one, unified.

His hands touched the wooden beams of the altar. He felt metal nails with the palms of his hands, and a prickling on his scalp. A sudden flash of pain went through his whole body, and he cried aloud, shutting his eyes. The agony went as soon as it had come, and he felt enraptured again as he looked at the soft dawn light unfolding in the land beneath. It was his birthday, he was twelve years old. He had been born in a stable, so they said, three days after the winter solstice, and he knew there had been much celebrating at his birth, but he was not sure why. It would become clear to him one day, no doubt.

He could hear voices from the foot of the Tor. The druids would be coming up soon, and the boy thought he had better walk down and leave them to perform their ceremonies. His feet brushed through the frosty grass leaving dark footmarks, and he delighted in making curved tracks, complex dark patterns on the white fields. He wondered if his family were thinking of him on this, his twelfth birthday, and what they were doing back in Nazareth; keeping warmer than he was, no doubt of that. He whistled as he strode down through the now sunlit fields, and wondered what was for breakfast.

The trouble with starting a new life in a new town is that you don't know anybody, and nobody knows you. You go off to work and get to know people there, then you come home to your family, and of course you know them, but who else? The problem is solved without thinking about it if you have children. They go off to school and meet new people, and these new people have brothers and sisters, and parents. They invite their new friends round to play after school, and parents come to fetch them, and all of a sudden you find that you know a lot of new people, parents of your children's friends. This is how it works.

The new house we had bought slowly turned into a home. In the Spring, the garden started to look green, and I dug bits of it over, sowed potatoes under black polythene, but left most of the area as rough meadow grass, which I mowed every week. The kids could play on it, with their friends, and although it was an uneven surface, cricket and football were easily accommodated on its forgiving carpet. We used to watch the chap next door who dug over his future lawn, by hand and then by rotivator (twice), then sieved, then rolled, then raked, then sowed with grass seed, then weeded meticulously by hand, then re-seeded, re-rolled, and so on. It took him two years. All the time we were playing games on ours, and laughing at him. But then, he had no kids. He never had a perfect lawn,though, since weeds, cats, birds and Nature always conspired to wreck his efforts.

We both went to Evening Classes, and met more newcomers to the Town. One was on the Roman history of the place, and was very good, and the other was an Art class, run by the art teacher at the local High School. This was excellent, and after a couple of years, we had got so used to one another that we decided to put on an exhibition at the local fire-station, where one of the women's husbands was a fireman. The proved a great success, and we got over two hundred artists to contribute works, which we hung on the whitewashed walls of the Fire station. It was my first introduction the the public life of Elcaster, and although we didn't sell many pictures, we got a lot of people in through the doors, and made a small but significant mark on the Town's map.

My own new job was not going nearly so well. I had taken the post of Head of Chemistry in a school in South Birmingham. It had been a Grammar School, and was struggling to cope with the comprehensive revolution that was sweeping the country, spearheaded by Birmingham, of all unlikely places. I did not like the school much, but I thought I could get on with the staff, most of whom had been there for many years, and who were almost unanimously opposed to comprehensives. I was wrong. I found them detestable.

I had only taught at one school in my life at this time. When I had finished my degree in polymer technology at the Northern Polytechnic, I decided long before I finished that the rubber industry was a Victorian relic with no prospects for the future. So I had to do something, and I found out that in 1960 you could go and teach Science without any other qualifications except a degree. You did not need to be trained, they were so short of scientists that they encouraged them to start in schools straight away. I had taken advantage of this in Swindon. a town full of London overspill families, working at the newly set-up industries like Pressed Steel and Plessey. I applied, got an interview with an elderly lady, who wanted me to start in a Grammar School, of which there were at least three in Swindon. I refused, saying that I wanted to find out quickly if I was suited to teaching, and I thought a Secondary Modern would give me that experience. I was still under the romantic influence of wanting to work with Real People, not carefully selected clever kids from middle-class homes. If I wanted an easy life, I could have taught in a private school but that was not my aim. So I started in September 1960 at Walcot Secondary Modern School.

I thrived from the outset. I found I was the only staff

member with a degree, albeit a strange one in polymers. It was a degree, however, and I got paid a little extra for having it. I was told before term started by the hulking Head of Maths that if I fitted in I would do well, if not, I would be 'out on my ear'. He must have been wary of me, public-school education with a science degree, this one might give himself airs above his station. This delivered in a broad Yorkshire accent with not a trace of a smile. It didn't scare me one little bit. I just felt right there, and I knew I could do it. Something to do with my Public School experiences, the confidence of youth. I was just 23, and had been married for two weeks.

It was a great school, full of very good teachers. I learned a lot from listening to them in the Staff Room at break and after school, across the smoke as we all relaxed and talked about the day's events. It was compulsory to go on the Staff Outing every month, on Friday night, at a nearby pub. No spouses were allowed, and no absences, even if you had been off sick. I know now that I was protected and encouraged by those older teachers, mostly men, who privately thought that teaching was the greatest job in the world, but were not going to say so out loud. They showed it every day in what they did. It was not a harsh school , but discipline was tight, and woe betide you if you stepped out of line with the other teachers. A united front was presented to the pupils, and the parents. There was little trouble. The parents, mostly Londoners, were glad to find a good school where their kids were as happy as could be expected at the start of the 60s. Male staff were expected to demonstrate that you could hit kids, mostly around the head. It was shown to me how to do it, roll your hand over the top of their heads and give a push so their head rocked sideways; it looked much worse than in fact it felt. You only had to show the Staff that you were capable of doing it once or twice, and you were accepted. I hated doing it, but it worked, it worked quickly, and it left no damage, or none that we could see. Most of the boys got far worse at home.

I modelled myself on one of the best teachers I had ever met, the biology teacher from my Public School, Humphrey Moore. I had been thinking about this for years, ever since I saw him for the last time, back when I was nineteen, and thought I knew it all. I had left school a year before, and we all went back to drink and be as stupid as Old Boys can be, and he hardly spoke to me. I hardly noticed. But his shade has travelled with me all this time, his mocking smile and sarcastic bite still live within me. I still try to gain his approval. I don't know why.

I dreaded going to my new public school before I went. I was well-read in Tom Brown's schooldays, and the like, and knew what to expect: bullying, more stern and loveless teaching, systematised brutality, and boys that had crushes on you and did nameless things to you until it was your turn to do the same nameless things to the New Sprogs.

I was mostly wrong. There was no bullying that I could

not easily surmount, and give as good as I got. Brutality was confined to cold showers as punishment, and no-one had a crush on me, so the nameless things never came around. But it was the teachers who were the greatest surprise to me. They regarded me as clever, and treated me as such. I got the second highest scholarship, so they just assumed that I was intelligent. This amazed me. No-one had ever treated me like that, except my mother. I was in Heaven. There was a huge library, with open fires, where we could spend almost the whole Sunday reading. And the evenings too. We were in the heart of Dorset, and were encouraged to walk out in the woods and fields. It was like Elysium to me.

They taught two sciences, and I took to Biology and Chemistry like a duckling to water. The chemistry teacher was mildly bohemian, artistic (he produced the school plays), and unthreatening. The biology teacher was the one who most reminded me of my past Prep School experiences. He had a reputation as a beater, and had a daunting and frightening air, menacing and grim. He cultivated this deliberately. He was a man with whom you did not mess, if you knew what was good for you. And I did, I did. No messing with Humphrey Moore, not at all.

I cannot lie and say I remember my first lesson with him, because I don't. I knew early on that I liked Biology, and after a few weeks, I liked Humph too; he joked and picked me out as a boy who could reply with passable wit to his amusing sarcasm. He was like some of my relatives, he liked quick repartee, and I was good at it. I began to think how unfair his reputation was; why, he was clever and kind, what could be nasty about such an uncle?

I found out after three months. I made some funny reply to one of his sallies, and like a striking cobra he rounded on me. "Get out," he croaked. "Go and report to the Head for rudeness." His eyes were hard and glittering, his mouth a gash of cruelty. He was enjoying my total shock. I felt mentally ambushed, cut to my very soul. It was the scene with Mr. Maurice all over again, just as I had felt safe and warm.

The Head, known as Bunter, was a genial buffoon, but who was a great deal smarter than most people gave him credit for. He hated caning, and luckily for me, he was incredibly bad at it. He mouthed some platitudes about 'scholarship boy, expect better,' but his heart wasn't in it; he knew Humph's tricks of old, and he knew I had been set up as an example to the others. He did not want me shot at dawn, so he whacked me on the back of the legs a few times, and blarted out some more phrases about buckling down and such. He was a kind man, and lit another cigarette and smiled at me before he let me go back to Biology.

Humph never mentioned it again, but he had shown his true nature. I never trusted him from that morning on. In the years to come I would interact with him a lot, but he could not be trusted, so I watched my back with him, always. That attitude stood me in good stead later, so I was grateful to him for showing his hand so soon. Even the nicest people can be horrible at times, especially when they have power. It was an important lesson I had learned when I got sent out by Humph. But I was very sore about it at the time.

I sailed on with little thought for the future, I was enjoying myself, as much as was possible in school. The place was organised like a farm, where the new boys at 13 went into the Junior House, looked after by 'Drip' Appleby, a benign elderly homosexual, who was relatively harmless to his charges. He encouraged my writing, allowing me (or anyone, I was not singled out) the freedom to write what I liked for homework. Epic Poems, stories, I tried to put down what I had read so greedily for the last six years. It was my first experience of artistic creation that attracted approval. Art was only a hobby there, since the teacher, Mr. Scadding, was the Chaplain, and God had given him permission to do next to nothing, so he that is what he did. This did no harm, but he was not in the least an inspirational man. He painted portraits of the pretty new boys and sold the works to adoring mothers; it made him pocket money, and they were not bad. But he was a lazy and selfish man, only mildly homosexual, as many of the bachelor staff were.

In your second year, you went up the The Middles, whose housemaster was Humphrey Moore. The building was the old stables of the Victorian house that housed the school. Humph, also called 'Creech', (as in Creature), and 'Uncle', ruled with an iron fist in an iron glove. It seemed to be agreed in the school that boys of 14 to 15 were trouble, and needed to have the Devil knocked out of them. Humph was the Devil-finder par excellence.

The day started and you had to strip your bedclothes back. If you failed to do this, you would be informed at breakfast of your crime, and beaten immediately afterwards. Humph was an expert at caning. He kept several canes, of different lengths and thicknesses, and used them wickedly. Many a boy had six bleeding cuts on his backside, all within millimetres of each other, but all separate. He always meant to cause pain, sometimes not too much.

His Middles prefects were his acolytes in maintaining tight discipline. Dirty shoes, insolence, untidy turnout (hard to be very untidy when the uniform was corduroy shorts and grey sweater), all were punished, often by a beating from the prefects themselves, with a sawn-off hockey stick. This made a lot of noise, but inflicted little pain beyond a stinging sensation.

I never got beaten by anyone after my session with Bunter. I gave up smoking, and could easily keep my nose clean. I never became one of anyone's Little Boys, though. I did not have the qualities of cheeky prettiness, and I was glad of that. One of my friends did, and it seemed at the time to do him little harm. It is only now that I wonder how unhealthy that Middles atmosphere was. Humph was a predatory homosexual, and could be vicious, as I had found. Overall, the Middles House ran smoothly, without too much fear and oppression, but I think that was my experience. Others with less confidence might have found it Hell on Earth. I was OK, that was all that mattered to me then.

Humph was a brilliant teacher of biology. The school had lots of microscopes, and we learned to use them early on. We looked at live amoebae, paramecium, hydra, cells of all kinds, and he could talk about the subject like no-one I had ever heard. It was magic to me, although I kept my mouth shut mostly; he liked questions, and would divert into areas of expertise in biology that were fascinating, but not on the O Level syllabus. He had a real passion for his subject, and could put it over in mind-gripping way, that no other teacher in the school could do.

Once a month we would have the Biology Test. This was done on a piece of A5 paper, and would be about 20 questions on the last month's work. It included all the hard words, and all the answers were in the notes he had given us. You revised for Humph's tests, because if you failed, you were beaten. No pass-mark, he just beat you if he thought your mark was too low. I used to do well, so I never got beaten, but there was a delicious undercurrent of danger to his tests. I loved them, and feared them. Some of the less able must have had nightmares about them, but there was no way out.

We had to attend Chapel once a day, and instead of a

sermon, staff used to read from books of their choice. Some were excruciatingly dull, but Humph always chose something interesting to me. 'A Glastonbury Romance' was one, and 'The Once and Future King,' the story of King Arthur by T.H.White, captured my imagination. Scadding read from 'The Little World of Don Camillo', so he went up in my estimation. He couldn't stop himself from laughing out loud as he was reading it, and had to take a few seconds to recompose himself.

The Physics staff were pathetic; one man had a mind like a rabbit-warren, and muddled you up in an instant. The other was a sour humourless suppressed homosexual, vicious and petty-minded, and we loathed each other. Most of the staff detested him too, that was evident even to me at 15, so they made little secret of their dislike. He was an appalling teacher, and I never liked physics until I was at College.

Humph was not only a teacher of biology, he was a scientist as well; he was researching toad migration. The school had a lake, and toads bred there. Every year in the Spring, on one particular night, thousands of toads would come from miles around to breed in the lake. They were squashed on the road in their dozens, so we always knew when they were migrating. Humph wanted to find out what triggered this, what made them rise up all on the same night. He had marked specimens, and knew what great distances they travelled.

I had helped in the Biology lab by looking after the tropical fish, even mending a tank with special putty, so Humph asked if I would like to stay up all night to measure the pH around the lake, to see if this had any correlation with the toads' behaviour. I chose a friend to help me, 'Dad' Hoare (so named because he used to call everyone 'son') from my old Prep School, who seemed likely to complete the task with me.

It was warm and we did the testing easily at first, using a torch to see the colour change in the solutions. About one in the morning, Dad Hoare got tired, and suggested we got a bit of kip, and made up the rest of the results, as they were not changing much. I was horrified at such an idea, but he just laid by a tree and told me to do it myself. So I did, without missing many, until about eight o'clock, when the experiment was to end. I can still remember struggling to keep my eyes open; the smell of wet marsh, the rising mist as dawn slowly crept up, and the weird noises of birds, the splash of fish, and Dad Hoare's snores. I felt like a pioneer at the Frontiers of Science. I was hooked. Thousands wrote; only a few discovered something truly new, and they were the Scientists, who would save the world. I felt tired but elated. Humph would be pleased, I thought. And so he was, he could see the light of conversion in my eyes; he was no fool.

We got on with the O Level stuff, and I learned to draw properly for the first time by sketching rabbit bones. You had to get in all the nuances of changes in contour, as well as correct proportions. I spent ages over getting them right, and I wish I had those drawings now. It taught me to really look hard before using the pencil. We drew insects, microscope slides, details of animals preserved in formalin, leaves, twigs, seeds. I did it all with gusto. It taught me infinitely more about the art of drawing than the lazy Scadding ever did.

We used to do Ecology, by walking out to various environments, some in the school, but most in the fields and chalk hills around. Hod Hill was the woodland environment, and I can recall still the fascination of seeing the evolutionary struggle laid out before us, silent and still, yet a struggle of life and death. Humph made it live for me. The countryside became so much more interesting to walk in now that I could see what was going on. It still is.

After three years there, I did very well at O Level. I took 10 subjects, and got them all, the only one in my year, and only the second person to get 10 in the school's history. O Level had only been going a few years, but the beady eyes of old Bunter fell on me. I was a potential Oxbridge candidate, except that I had given up Latin, at last, to my relief. I had a struggle with Bunter, but he relented as he realised that I would not change. "Ah well, I suppose redbrick will have to do," he sighed.

I went into the sixth form, choosing sciences and maths in preference to the Arts. It was a hard choice, because I did love writing and literature, but science seemed so much more useful in the little matter of earning a living. My father's business had gone bust, and my parents went to keep a pub. I did not want to find myself in my father's position at any time in my life.

Physics was deadly dull, chemistry was OK, but biology was fast. We were going to do it in one year so that we could do Botany and Zoology as two subjects the following year. I had become a Priv., a sort of sub-prefect, and I was very disappointed. Some of my friends had become prefects, and I wanted to be one too. I was competitive. I wanted authority and power, the marks of Success. I was Sergeant of No. 1 Platoon in the CCF, why not a prefect?

I joined the Arts Society, a weekly meeting in the rooms of 'Drip' Appleby at eight in the evening. We drank China tea, and read out our poems, displayed our paintings, for we had to bring some thing of our own for some of the meetings. At others we brought works of Art that moved us. My friend Ed worshipped T.S.Elliot, so we argued about the Waste Land. Once Ed brought 'Rock Island Line' by Lonnie Donegan. Drip was unconvinced that it was High Art, but Humph said he liked it, just to annoy Drip, I think. He was like that, playfully mischievous in his best moods, downright unpredictably nasty in others. Many of the people at those meetings were studying Sciences, and Humph could certainly hold his own in discussions about any aspect of the arts. I never questioned that scientists should get involved in painting, writing, or whatever. It struck me then that many Arts people hardly know a thing about science. It is their loss, since science is so much part of the culture. It occurred to me then that Arts people are sometimes not as bright as scientists. I still think that, with fifty years experience.

I was rewarded in my search for authority after one term. Humph asked me if I would be a Middles Prefect, and I jumped at the chance. My friend Bob had been one for a term, and I shared a room with Khadji, from Persia, a fellow Biology student, who was to become a surgeon in the future.

I got on well with Humph. He was laid back, not at all what he seemed to be when I was a lad of 15 in his house. He turned a blind eye to our trips to local pubs (not too local, naturally), and to the drinking in the studies that went on after the youngsters had been put to bed. My friend Ed had weekly parcels from his father, the head brewer of Watney's Stag Brewery, which were mostly bottles of Stingo, a very strong ale. Some drank Merrydown Cider, and other ghastly alcoholic drinks. We had a lot of freedom, we were trusted not to abuse it, and we didn't. For a while, it was the best time of my life.

It was after I had had to beat a small boy called Cox, with squinting eyes behind his pebble glasses, that I realised that this was not my style. I liked the business of telling people what to do, but not the punishment part. I started to dislike the idea of Public School life. I mixed with ordinary people in the holidays, in the Public Bar of the Salutation Inn at Faringdon, and I saw the life of the Public School boy, my life, as an undeserved privilege. I wanted out. I wanted to Earn my Living by the Sweat of my Brow, amongst the People. I was not going to University, more Privilege for the Rich. There were companies advertising for Trainees, to get degrees as well as experience on the factory floor. That was for me, I decided. But how to get out, with only one more year to go, when my parents had spent all this money on my education? It was assumed by Bunter that I would go to a top University, and hints that I might not went down like a lead balloon.

I mentioned this to my mother in the Easter holidays. She said, "Oh, don't worry about wasting our money. Granny has been paying the school fees all along!" This revelation decided me. I owed no loyalty to Granny, nice person though she was. I told my father as I went back for the Summer Term that I would not be doing another year. It was possible that I would be Head Boy, and I dreaded the thought. All that responsibility and speechmaking, it just wasn't me.

The dung hit the fan when Bunter found out. Humph was noncommittal, he knew some of my doubts were based on my newly-emerging beliefs, and would not easily be shifted. My father was summoned down by Bunter, who completely convinced him that on no account should I be allowed to leave, I had a great future ahead, blah, blah, blah. Bunter was good at that kind of thing, being a Tory agent for Dorset, and my Dad was no match for his silver tongue.

I met my Dad in the front porch, and he started to explain to me that I had to stay on for my own good, when Humph came up to us. Humph hated parents, he was utterly embarrassed, especially with the mothers, and he turned and twisted when talking to them, like a fish on dry land. But he took my father off for a walk round the grounds, his strange square-shaped head at its usual angle on his neck, tilted away from Dad. But he must have talked well. He made my old man see that it was best to let me go my own way, my time in an Institution was over, and I would only get unhappy again, as I had been at my Prep School. I never found out what he said exactly, but it worked. The main telling point he told Dad was that I was too intelligent not to get a degree, but that a break now would do me good, focus my mind on what I wanted to do, and I would be the better for it. And he also said that Bunter was a well-meaning buffoon, with his eyes only on the benefits to the school.

Humph got me my freedom. He had come along 'by accident', as he said later, the old liar, and he wished me well. I had some uncharitable suspicions that he wanted to get shot of me because I might spill the beans in the wrong quarters about his homosexuality, but if that was his motive, he never let on. It never bothered me anyway, until after I had left. It still doesn't much.

I passed my A Level Biology, getting a Distinction for my dissection of the cranial nerves of the dogfish. What luck we didn't get the frog, the rabbit, or the cockroach; we got the only one we had studies in detail! Humph cheated? Surely not!

For much of my four years at the school, I wanted to please Humphrey Moore more than any of the other teachers, some of whom were excellent, some less so. I was more than a little afraid of his rejection for all that time, and he was certainly unpredictable as a person. Not as a teacher, though. He had good and bad days in the classroom, but his interest in his subject always shone out. He laughed when he put two harmless snakes on the table for me to keep from falling off, but if the snakes had been in danger, he would have protected them. I could look after myself.

I think I wanted his approval because he was in many ways the kind of person that I wanted to become. I wanted to be able to study many subjects intelligently, and be able to talk about them. I wanted to be the kind of person who was not always the same, who could get wiser, who could understand difficult ideas. Of course, I wanted a lot of other things as well. I wanted children, a wife, a good time, but those were externals, results of me being who I wanted to be. I did not want the unkindness, having people fear me, the patent loneliness of the man.

So when I became a teacher five years later, having got

my degree and married my wife, I had no doubt which teacher I would model myself on. I taught in a Secondary Modern School in Swindon, quite unlike a Public School in Dorset, but I had few doubts that I could do it. All schools have something in common, they contain kids. I had dozens of models to totally reject, my prep school had given me plenty of examples of how not to do it. But I wanted to be like Humph, with a bit less fear and a bit more tolerance. I used the monthly test, the occasional sarcasm, the unpredictability to keep them on their toes, and I loved my subject, or most of it.

Later on, when I left teaching to go and do research and development, I called Humph to mind again. He had the right mixture of playfulness and knowledge to research his toads, and I could see that if you took research too seriously you would never do anything of any merit. Richard Feynman, the American atomic scientist, must have been a bit like Humphrey, I think. Not always the most popular of people, but playing with ideas was his strength.

In some ways he could be as horrid as some of the worst teachers that I had at my Prep school. He had plenty of faults as a human being. He was not nice, or always kind, he was no cuddly Mr. Chips, beloved by all. He made an impression on boys, he could never be called an insipid character. There must be many who remember him as a hated and feared figure, and probably some whose emotional life he wrecked permanently. He should not be forgiven for that.

Teachers take that risk, though, at boarding schools. Parents take the risk by sending their children to such schools where the people who take their place are not always good or kind. Neither are parents, of course. He showed me that to be taught by someone, you don't have to like them. You can even fear them a little, as long as you do not hate or despise them. I tried to remember that as a teacher myself.

Humph would have found it impossible to do some of the teaching that I have done, with pupils who are none too bright, with disruptive kids, in schools with appalling management, and little support for the teachers. He would not indeed have done it at all. His methods could only work inside the public school system, with tacit approval by all, including parents, of the methods of discipline. Like all minor public school figures, he was probably an authoritarian, believing in rule by the elite, and to hell with the underclasses, they should be put in their place. That is the public school ethos, and it seeps into you slowly but persistently. It did not take in me, because I was a dissenter. But I loved the life at the time, it was good for me, yet I rejected it in the end. That ethos was embedded in me though, I didn't rid myself of it all at once, it took years, and even now some of it remains. What you do at a young age stays with you, and it has made my life quite uncomfortable at times. But the authoritarian ethos is there, and it was very seductive to the individual, as mild fascism always is. This country will always be backward so long as private education of the ruling elite continues.

But whatever Humph's politics were, they meant nothing in the context of the school at the time. He would not have done at all well in a State School, under inspection by OFSTED. He had no Lesson Plan, no Schemes of Work, nothing that wasn't in his head, or in the syllabus. But he had the greatest quality a teacher can have. He could inspire. And he did, for he inspired me, by hook, by crook, by death and damnation, as well as by example. May he rest in peace, he was a damn good teacher, and I wish that I had half his gift.

I never intended to go back as an Old Boy, except once. Those who left in 1955 all agreed to come back on Old Boys Weekend and have one last extravagant binge. We did that, and I have always remembered that feeling we all had, of being Men of the World at last, and I'm afraid we behaved badly, myself as badly as anyone. I wrote this letter in 2011 to explain why I wasn't going to another Old Boys celebration, ever.

SarahJane Newland,
The Development Office,
Clayesmore School,
Iwerne Minster,
Dorset DT11 8LL

Dear Ms. Newland,

Congratulations on your new-look Old Clayesmorian. I am grateful to be still on your mailing list.

Reading it, I was wondering why I do not contribute. I was at Clayesmore from 1951–1955, and loved it. It gave me independence of mind, amongst lots of other qualities, and I shall be forever thankful I went there. But after four years as a pupil, I wanted to join the Real World, and left to work for Avon Tyres. Yes, I was that romantic, and in some ways I still am; Clayesmore never knocked that out of me, thank Goodness. To this day, I dislike overbearing authority, and Clayesmore never gave me any to rebel against. Humphrey Moore was the sternest, but I modelled my teaching methods on him when I started teaching science in a Secondary Modern in 1960. Mr. Spinney and 'Drip' Appleby were wonderful eccentric teachers, and nobody could ever rebel against 'Bunter' Burke, he was just too benevolent.

But we used to despise the Old Boys who came down regularly. They seemed to have no lives, and just wanted to relive the only times they had been happy. We did not want to be like them, so before we left, we made a pact. We would come back on one weekend in the summer after we left, in 1956, and have a whale of a party, see each other for the last time, and go our respective ways.

We did that. I know I ought to be ashamed of the hooliganish way we behaved, but sadly I am not. It was wild. I woke up on the Sunday in the room over the Middle's Arch, and found I had thrown up into the wastepaper basket. I washed it out, and tipped it out of the window, I have no idea why. By Fate's dread hand, Mr. Daniels, the Physics teacher, was passing beneath. He assumed that I had done it on purpose, and I was the only Old Boy told that weekend never to darken the doors of Clayesmore again. I did not mind. That was our pact, after all. I did get a letter a few years later saying all was forgiven (not by Mr. Daniels, no doubt), and I have been back quietly several times since, and admired the new additions. My 15 year-old granddaughter came with me last year, and thought it "very posh, Papa". It didn't seem so at the time, but it was comfortable. I thought it a beautiful place, and it still is.

Maybe I shall look more kindly on Old Boys, and Girls, in the future. But somehow I doubt it.
You may publish this or not, you are the Editor. I just thought you might be interested.

Yours sincerely,
Jonathan 'Bill' Bayley, ex Middle's Prefect

I had taken the post in Birmingham because I was disastrously short of money. I could not pay my weekly bills on a classroom teacher's salary, so I got promotion to Head of Chemistry. I knew I had made a mistake the moment I walked into the Staff room. I was approached by a bulky woman, who introduced herself as Mrs. Peabody, Head of Mathematics. Her first question put me ill at ease. "Which University did you go to? I'm a Cambridge Graduate myself. I'm the Deputy Head."

I recognised the trap. Snobbery rules applied. Too bad. "I got my degree at the Northern Polytechnic, Holloway Road, London. In polymer science. I have also worked in industry. Have you?"

She saw the battle lines being drawn at once. Her already rocklike face hardened; she made a half-polite noise, and turned away. I saw her surrounded by toadies, and watched as they looked over their shoulders at me. I was left isolated. How different from my last dear school, Walcot. No support here for teachers, only cut-throat internal politics. And how right I proved.

The Head was an ass. He also had a degree from Cambridge, in the Classics, and he taught a little Greek to the Sixth Form. He was completely in the pocket of the malevolent Mrs. Peabody. He knew nothing of what went on in his school, apart from the lies she told him. The other Staff were weak and subservient to her. She ruled the school with a rod of iron, bullying the staff and the pupils in the same callous way.

The first Staff meeting revealed the ethos of the place.

The first item was about the Admissions Policy. The eleven-plus had been abolished, but some schools, including this one, St. Stephen's, were allowed to set an entrance paper. There was an Admissions Committee, chaired of course by Mrs. Peabody, with two sycophants with her. It became clear that those pupils let in were from the schools approved by Mrs. Peabody, and other schools had no input at all. Latin was a part of the test, and was only taught at those schools Mrs. Peabody was in close contact with. The whole set-up was even more corrupt than the Eleven-plus, but nobody dared say so. It was the exact opposite of why I had come into education. St. Stephen's taught a stuffy syllabus to a privileged few. I knew my days there were numbered.

I brought up the fact that Chemistry was only taught to the top third of the school, and in my experience, it should be taught to all, with a suitable syllabus. My suggestion fell into a dark and silent pit. Mrs. Peabody looked through her pince-nez at me. "And just what is your experience at teaching the ...er... less intelligent pupils, Mr. Bayley? I see you taught General Science at a...Secondary Modern School in...Swindon." She almost spat her contempt of the concepts she plainly despised.

"Yes, I have considerable experience at teaching the less able. I believe Chemistry can be taught to anyone, given the right approach."

She drew her massive bosom in. "You have no experience around here, though. I think we have more idea of what approach to take than you may think you have." She then went on to the next item. I had been completely shut out.

I had no input into the Science syllabus. The Head of Science was a feeble old snob who always thought Mrs. Peabody was right. He spoke to me afterwards.

"Mr. Bayley, you have a lot to learn. This is not a Secondary Modern, it is a Grammar School in all but name, and we intend to uphold our long-established principles, no matter what any Government may dictate. And you must realise that Tradition always takes precedence over Modernity here. New ideas are just not welcome. You had better remember that." He turned and shuffled away like a malicious old mole.

I found few friends at that school. The only ones that agreed with me in any way were the Lab Technicians, the caretaker, and the school secretary. I asked one why they had appointed me, as I was so obviously a fish out of water. "Oh, that's easy. You went to a Public School, that's why. They assumed you would be as Tory as they are. They were a bit off-beam, weren't they?" The Head Lab Tech was a nice girl, working at getting her Open University degree so she could go and teach. "And not in a dump like this one, either. They're all half dead or on the right of Ghengiz Khan. Poor kids!"

Poor kids indeed. Only the top third were considered 'bright enough' for the staff to bother teaching them at all.

They had a chance of getting in to a 'Top University', although very few actual did. They had never got anyone to Oxbridge, but that didn't stop them talking as if they did. The lower seventy percent were written off as 'thick', and left to go to low-class Universities, Polytechnics, or even worse, to train as engineers or managers in local industries. These were bored to distraction with the dull pap presented to them as 'Education', and they couldn't wait to leave. This did not lead to any discipline problems, quite the contrary. The school had the whip hand, and ruthlessly expelled anyone who was out of line. For some reason beyond my comprehension, St. Stephen;s had a high reputation amongst parents and employers, and there was competition to get in. I wouldn't have let my own children within a mile of the place, so should I be teaching there?

I needed the money, so I had to grit my teeth and get on with it. The actual teaching was easy, since the standard in the school was abysmally low. They had only had above-average pupils to cope with for years, and they would put up with the tosh doled out to them by the dull teaching staff. So my kingdom became my classroom, and what went on outside was of little interest to me. I never liked schools much at that time, they always seemed to be cumbersome hierarchies run by incompetent pomposities, with always the wrong people in charge, but where else but a school would you find children in enough numbers to earn a living by teaching? But I kept on brushing up against Mrs. Peabody. My Head of Science left me alone, as he could see I was a better teacher than he was, and was capable of defending myself should he attack. Doubtless he moaned about me to La Peabody, but she was a different calibre. She had Authority, and I was defying it. I had to be Corrected.

She tried at first to immolate me with bureaucracy. I was wise to that, and avoided her clumsy attempts. But I had no friends in the Staff room, so I was no threat to her supremacy. We had sparring matches often, but she never found a chink in my armour. Until one day I got too overconfident.

It was over such a trivial matter, but most school quarrels are. Teachers are peculiarly petty, and she picked up a comment I made in a Staff meeting. The building was in poor condition, and the chemistry lab had a leak in the drainage system, which dripped waste which was possibly toxic onto the benches of the lab below. I had asked for something to be done about this for weeks, and nothing happened. So I mentioned in the Staff meeting that I might write to the papers saying how poorly maintained Birmingham Schools were. She looked calmly at me, and asked to see me in he study afterwards.

I went and knocked at her door, and was asked by her secretary to return in the morning, at 9.00 am precisely. So I did. I went in to find the Headmaster, La Peabody and a man in a black suit sitting in a row behind her desk.

"Ah, Mr. Bayley." She was at her smoothest, her most

dangerous. "You made a threat to damage the reputation of St. Stephen's yesterday. No use denying it, the whole staff heard you. What have you to say? By the way, this is Mr. Robson, the school lawyer. He will be taking down your answer." I was speechless. All this for a suggestion I might write a letter?

"I have nothing to say. The drain should have been repaired, it's a threat to health. I merely wanted to speed up the process."

"No doubt you did. That is not the point. It specifically states in your Conditions of Employment that you may not communicate with outside agencies about anything that happens in a school in which you are employed. Do I make myself clear?"

Eminently. I was being set up for at least a written reprimand. I said nothing.

She continued. "You will receive a written reprimand, which will appear on your record of employment. If you wish to appeal, that is your right. Are you in a Union?" A chink of light!

"Yes, Mrs. Peabody, I am in the NUT. I shall appeal to them."

Her little piggy eyes glinted. I had made another mistake. "Excellent, You are aware that both the Head and myself are also in that same Union? It will be your word against ours. You have a record of unwise statements, you know."

I was beaten. She was using the petty rules of

Birmingham Education Authority against me. She knew them backwards, and I did not. I could not win. I left the office feeling extremely angry, but powerless. I heard her humourless laugh behind me as the door closed. That old fool the Head had not said a word.

My luck changed in the next week. I ran into an old college friend in a pub round the corner. He had been working for Lusac Aerospace, I knew, and asked him how it was going. "Great! There's jobs going in the labs, if you want. But I suppose you're wedded to your academic life, aren't you. The pay is brilliant, by the way. I don't suppose your is!" He was right there. It seemed like a heaven-sent chance to spike Mrs. Peabody's guns.

My wife was enthusiastic. she could tell St Stephen's did not suit me at all, and she could see more money would come in useful with three children at school.

So I applied, and got the job. The pay was an increase of 50%, a massive amount which made me realise how out-of-touch I had become with the Real World of Work. All that remained was the thoroughly pleasant task of telling the Head I was leaving at Easter, after only two terms at his shoddy little school. It could not have gone better. Mrs. Peabody was also there when I handed the Head my month's notice, the minimum required. His eyes popped as he read the letter, and he handed it to La Peabody, as if he didn't know what to do, which he probably didn't.

She scrutinised it through her pince-nez. Her ugly head shot up. "You can't do this, you know, You can't leave us in the middle of an academic year. You must wait until the end of the Summer term. How can we get a replacement at this short notice?"

But I had read my Conditions of Employment by this time. "You'll find I only have to give one months notice. There it is. My replacement is your problem. Good-day.' She started to splutter, "You'll not work in this Authority again! With your written warning, I shall see to it!"

I turned and faced her. "Are you threatening me with unfair practices, Mrs. Peabody? I think you'll find that what you are suggesting is illegal, and certainly not covered by the Conditions of Employment. Once again, Good-day." And I swept out, laughing inwardly. This time there was silence from the Head's study.

They never even gave me a leaving present, although the kids did. I shook the dust of St. Stephen's off my feet with disdain, sorry to leave teaching, but realising that not all schools are the same. I had learned a valuable lesson. Or so I thought.

STEP THREE -- STARTING OFF

As I promised you earlier in this book you won't find instructions about How to Run A Youth Club here. At least, not yet. I am trying to set the scene for you, to show how a person who has the strange desire to run a youth club is constructed, how he arrives at that off-centre point of departure. Like psychopaths, they are neither entirely born nor made. They evolve, through a tortuous path of unlikely happenings and situations, combined with inherited genes, to emerge at the end with that abnormal, almost twisted, desire. And not just to have that desire, they must have the wish to continue, to persevere in the face of all the doubts and setbacks he will encounter, his own being the most powerful.

Nobody will stop him. Running a youth club is not like a murder or a robbery, it is not socially repellent. But nobody will encourage him either. People do not know what to say. They know it is not actually dangerous, nor completely foolhardy. It is a bit like someone saying, "I want to be a priest", or "I think I will join the Salvation Army". It is considered odd in the extreme, and most people have the immediate fear that they may be asked to help. They have their excuses all ready, of course. "I'm too busy," "I don't really want to mix with teenagers", "I'm allergic to acne," all perfectly valid. A few may look you in the eye, and say "Are you mad? Have you any idea what it involves?", but they are rare. They realise that for you to suggest you want to run a youth club is itself a symptom of a madness so complete, so devastating, that they have nothing to say. They can only mentally wring their hands and weep for you.

It obviously does not require academic qualifications, nor any intellectual prowess. This is why you never hear of any genius running one. Einstein was not known to have ever entered one, nor Bertrand Russell, nor any Nobel Prize-winner that I can think of. (I have Googled this, and I think I am on strong ground here). You do not start a youth club expecting to become a Celeb, unless you are a paedophile, and you won't be a Celeb, you will merely be Notorious, and in prison before you can say 'Jack Robinson's Trousers', which I am told is what notorious paedophiles say a lot, especially in front of Jack Robinson.

I do not know what qualities are needed to run a youth club. This must seem a strange statement coming from a man who has spent the last thirty-three years trying, on and off, to run one. But there it is. I have never met anyone else who set out to run one, at least, as an unpaid volunteer. I have met plenty of paid workers, and mainly the reasons they do it are the same reasons that drive people to do any job -- money and ability to do it well enough to get paid. Some of these people have been splendid to work with, others not so much. But that is how work is, good and bad. But why did I do it as a kind of vocation? I really have no idea. I am hoping that writing this will explain myself to myself. Nothing else will, I'm sure.

When I left teaching to join the Great British Industry, my first reaction was one of relief. I could leave the job behind when I left work, there was no marking (not that I had done much, but there were other tasks to be completed by morning). There was a different hierarchy, no pompous teachers to ego-massage. There were different kinds of people to work with, coming from all ends of the social spectrum.

Teaching had always seemed to be relentlessly middle-class, with few teachers from either end. I had been told at St. Stephen's that we were there "to promote middle-class values, as those are universally acclaimed to be the best." I had to leave this cretinous statement where it lay, unfortunately. It was made by the fatuous Head, of course, at a start-of-term staff meeting, and I knew without looking round that all the staff would be nodding wisely in agreement, soaked as they were in apathy and the puny class-ridden dogmas that comprised much of Education in those days. So nothing changes much.

I missed the kids, I knew I would, but I had my own three at home, and I was fresh enough in the evenings to be able to make up stories and play games, which I could not do after a day's teaching. It drained you, especially in St. Stephen's Gradgrind Academy. I was glad that my own children would not be cursed with having both parents as teachers, all of us embroiled in the silly tangles that schools generate. I could talk of another world, beyond the blackboard and the burden of homework, and give them a wider perspective on How Things Are.

But after three months I realised that something was missing from my life, something very valuable that I had had when teaching, and had now vanished. It came to me one night, as I was telling them one of the endless stories I made up about Mr. Splinkett and his dog Porky. It was creativity. There was none for me at work now. Most of the tasks I got through in the day were mundane and repetitive, and the people were pleasant enough, but dull. I felt that cold finger on my neck again, the Hand of Boredom, my worst terror. I was not that creative as a teacher, I had thought, but I did have my audiences, and I used to think about how to present the science to them, as much to interest me as them. When a teacher gets bored with his subject, time to quit, I had always thought. That was what was wrong at St. Stephen's, the teachers were bored with themselves, their subjects, and the pupils. No wonder they performed so badly.

The answer also came to me suddenly. I would take up painting seriously. I had always done a bit, gone to night schools, painted some pictures for the kids' bedrooms, even sold a few to friends. But now I was free in the evenings, I could paint until late at night, after the kids had gone to bed, and go on until two o'clock, and still be fresh enough to do the rather dull work expected of me at Lusac. So that was what I did, and it worked very well. Painting satisfied that creative urge that all artists have, and if the urge is not satisfied, they have some kind of reaction, usually a bad one. I had not realised that I had it until I gave up teaching. I had never thought of teaching as a creative art, but of course it is. Nobody can tell you how to teach, there are no instruction manuals for it. It is an art, and I had not realised it.

The new job itself was undemanding and straightforward. There were mutterings about an expansion into new technology, but this never got off the ground. The company, Lusac, was part of an old Birmingham group which had grown with the car industry. During the war, the fuel pump division had been tasked with designing a fuel system for the newly-invented gas turbine engine, top secret and highly innovative. The engineers worked superbly together, as Birmingham engineers can, and the first gas turbine engine made by Rolls Royce flew with a Lusac fuel system. This was developed and expanded into civil airliners, and Lusac were famous for their unique pumping methods. Unfortunately, as was common after the war, there was little money to invest properly, and the Americans took over making most of the jet engines in airliners. Rolls Royce and Lusac still made military engines, and were paid to develop these, but again the money ran out, bureaucracy stifled much innovation, and by the time

I joined Lusac, the accountants had gained control. This always means death to a high-tech industry, as accountants understand nothing except numbers, because they have zero vision. The good old engineers were sidelined, put out to grass, and the Cult of the Managers infected the whole company, as it infected the whole of British Industry. At the same time, or maybe because of this, the Trades Unions became more powerful, and stifled what tiny areas of life there were still left in the company. The whole place was like a dying whale when I went there; a once-glorious beast whose time had come, but nobody realised what was happening.

So the promises that I had been made when I applied for the job faded and died. Another sad fact became apparent. The old managers, who had all been first-class engineers, had had no skill at all in appointing successors. They promoted yes-men, third-raters who lauded themselves in getting a top job, but they had not had to work for it. They were almost entirely useless as managers, or as technical personnel. But they knew what they had to do all right -- "I've got a manager's badge, and I'll damn well manage!". They did immense harm. They had no knowledge of how systems work, what to change and what to leave alone, so they changed what should have been left, and left what should have been changed. This was the dreadful crime that was committed, and was at its worst in Birmingham. Brummies are some of the best engineers and innovators in the world, but only if they work for themselves. They have far too much respect for the Boss. In the old days, when Brummagem was being built, the Boss knew his stuff, and acted on it; he deserved respect. But after the war, Birmingham got flabby, imported American ideas, listened to politicians, allowed unions to gain too much power. It was Brummies who allowed this to happen, out of mistaken respect for the idiots who now were in charge. It lost us our manufacturing industry; cars, motorbikes, aircraft, electronics, railways, ships, pottery, guns, need I go on? I was trapped in a dead zone, highly paid, but with no discernible future. What should I do?

I did what most people did then. I carried on. The work was mundane, there was no spirit in the place, but this was the Seventies, everyone was in the same boat. Was teaching any better? My experiences had shown me that it was not much. So I stayed put. I felt a bit sorry for the men who had been in Lusac for years, and knew it when it had vision, and looked after its workers. I didn't trust it from my first day, and so I was not surprised or disappointed when Lusac turned out to be like all the rest, and started to make redundancies.

The atmosphere changed overnight. From being an easy-going and relaxed place to work, it became competitive and backbiting. Everyone was afraid for their job, and hugged the secrets of what they did to their tiny bosoms. It was a bit pathetic to see, as those chosen to go had nothing to do with how well they worked, it was more or less 'last in, first out'. Naturally, those who excelled at their jobs got new ones elsewhere, leaving the third-raters to carry on. There were plenty of those, since when Lusac was wealthy it wasn't too fussy about who it took on, and there was a whole forest of dead wood. But the worst aspect was that managers were protected, they dismissed mostly workers and technicians. This meant there was a small army of managers without anything to manage, so they meddled about even worse than ever. The process was called 'slimming down'. In practice, it was as if the slimmer had cut off limbs and hoped to work better than ever. Of course, the reverse occurred, and the Aerospace Division of Lusac went into a steep dive, from which it never recovered. And so did many companies at that time, for the same reason. Sheer incompetent management.

How glad I was that I had decided years before that management was not for me. I had discovered this fact when I was at my public school, in my final year. I really wanted to be a Prefect there, with authority and status. After one term in the Sixth Form, I got what I wanted. I was made a prefect. I had more authority in that role than I have ever had before or since. I could order younger boys around, sentence them to all kinds of punishments i.e. cold baths, detentions, shoe-cleaning, and even beat them with a sawn-off hockey stick, with the house-masters approval.

I thought I would love it. Everyone else did. But I hated it. I had to beat one small snivelling boy for not doing something trivial, and he was terrified. I shut my eyes, and performed the deed, despising myself as I did so. The image of my old prep-school head, Mr. Maurice, came into my mind. I was now no better than he was, the bully. I never beat another boy.

But I had learned something of great use to me, although I didn't realise it at the time. I did not believe in Management. Authority, yes, if it has earned respect. But people can manage themselves, they don't need someone else to do it for them. They might need teaching, correcting, encouraging, co-ordinating, even supervising for a time, but one human being does not 'manage' another. That's just another name for slavery. Even children are not 'managed'; they are taught. How they are taught varies, and punishment is not out of the question. But they are people even at a young age, and deserve respect and the allowance of as much freedom as is sensible.

So I was easily able to avoid the avalanche of bad management that flooded Lusac Aerospace. You just played one off against another, or ignored them entirely. But working conditions had certainly deteriorated massively. Our Lab manager, a very good man who never interfered with you unless he thought you were lazy or stupid, had gone to start another division. He had always been set against Trade Unions, so we weren't in a union in our lab. It was clear that we had better join one or we would be decimated in the next redundancies, because the managers sacked those who would make the least fuss. We couldn't make much fuss without support, so we joined a white-collar union. I was elected shop-steward, against my better judgement, but it was unanimous. They said "You are best at arguing, so you've got to do it." I couldn't deny I liked a good row, so I did the job.

It was dreadful. I had to join a shop-steward's committee of other departments, mostly old engineers, who had been trades unionists since they were babies, and really did address each other as 'Brother'. They did everything by the book, with minutes of meetings, putting motions to the meeting, convoluted language, everything that was parodied about them by Peter Sellars was accurate. Except that they were truly nice people, not greedy self-seekers at all, but they proceeded at the pace of a paralysed snail. The meetings were in North Birmingham on a Sunday. I went to three, and never went again. They sent me minutes of their wamblings, and I nodded to them, but it was a total waste of my time. Luckily, I was relieved of my post after the next Summer holiday. When I came back, nobody would look me in the face. I asked my mate Dave what was up. Shamefaced, he told me that a certain creep from another union had recruited them all the week after I went in holiday, and they thought I would be upset. Upset? I was delighted!

I did go on a three-day course at Birmingham University on Industrial Relations, paid for by the old union. Better than working, I thought, but little did I know about Union courses. All the others on the course were shop stewards from metal foundries, heavy engineering, and they were tough and brutal. This didn't bother me, although I wondered how Industrial Relations could improve with such hardened bigots in the union, but when we got onto the subject of Race Relations, I had a shock. I knew Brummies were supportive of Enoch Powell and his 'Rivers of Blood' speech, so I assumed our lecturer would be of a like mind, and tell us not to get involved with the Blacks, and how to legally avoid it. Not at all. He was very liberal, and started to tell the assembled hard men that they had to be more tolerant, that Pakistanis were as good workers as British, and so on. He only got ten minutes into his lecture when the scowling unionists cut him short. They told him he was wrong. Pakis were out to take over our jobs, our communities and our women, it says so in the papers, and if he hadn't anything better to say, he could f*ck off. He took the hint, and went. To my eternal shame, I remained silent. I hadn't got the nerve to argue with these Horny-handed Sons of Labour. After all, they were in the front line, and no coloured people worked at Lusac (it was 'company policy', even though illegal). They snarled and grumbled amongst themselves like hungry dogs, until a union man came in and ....apologised for the previous speaker! I was dumbfounded, but the hungry dogs were appeased. After all, they knew they were right. Everyone thinks so. I went home as soon as I could, vowing never to join another union as long as I lived.

The work I had to do got duller and duller. I went to my Chief Chemist with the outlines of four schemes we could get started. It wouldn't take much time, and I had plenty to spare. He was a nervous man, entirely unsuited to management, and he scanned my ideas, and said, "I don't think I could get permission, Bill."

"But you are Chief Chemist, Stan, whose permission do you need? Are you a man or a mouse? Have a bit of backbone, take a decision on your own!" This speech went through my head, but I didn't utter it. What would be the point? He was a mouse, all of them were, frightened for their jobs, lacking in any kind of personal vision, watching their backs. I decided after that to do more painting at home, late into the night when I wanted, and make up for the lack of sleep by kipping in the toilets for an hour or two each day. They'd never miss me. And sure enough, they never did.

I was having to make adjustments to my Life Plans by this time. I had already been through my first Mid-Life Crisis on my thirtieth birthday, on the stony beach at Littlehampton one Summer holiday, as I watched my three little children play happily in the sea. I was going nowhere, I had little money, none of the things that I assumed I would have done by now had happened, and here I was , a failure, with three kids to support for the next 15 or 20 years. Tears, real ones, trickled down my face. But I started properly from that moment to question my own assumptions. Who had told you what you would be doing? If you want a management job, why haven't you applied for one? Who is the judge of failure, you or others? Where had these ideas come from?

I slowly came to the conclusion that all these ideas

about myself and my so-called Career had come from others, not myself. Others such as prep-school and public school teachers, parents, friends, relatives, media, books. Everywhere except my own head. So it was that at the advanced age of thirty-one, I began to throw out the whole concept of a Career. After all, I had had two so far, one in teaching and one in industry, and both had paid me quite well. My father had once told me that a chap should be settled in his career by the age of thirty, and an hour later, it had dawned on me that he himself had done nothing of the kind, so where did that idea come from? Probably from his own teachers and parents. But they were as wrong about him as he was about me. So chuck away these outdated concepts, and decide for yourself! Easier said than done. Twelve years of brainwashing in private education is not shed so lightly. But the bonds had loosened. Of that there was no doubt. The Plan of my Life became more like an abstract painting, hard to decipher what was happening, but the main question was "does it look good?" It did.

My kids were growing, and doing well. They all seemed bright enough, and enjoyed family life, as far as I could tell. My son joined the cubs in a nearby village, because his friend had joined. His friend's father Glen and I were good friends too, and we were persuaded to join the Committee, to help raise funds for the cub pack. It was clear that this was a social position, and in the first year we spent at least twenty hours putting on a fete that raised thirty pounds. Glen and I discussed this and decided our time was being wasted in the company of dullards, and if we put an effort in we could raise much more, and enjoy ourselves as well. We put on a huge barbecue in a field nearby, as one of the other fathers was a farmer, and had always wanted to put on such an event. We went to town, spent a lot of money on advertising, good quality food, a steel band, amusements, an outside bar with Real Ale, all without consulting the Committee at all. The barbecue was a great success, raising over £400 in one night, and we had had a good time. We had mortally offended the Committee members, though, many of whom never spoke to either of us again. We were delighted. No more boring meetings to decide who runs the Tombola.

A surprise awaited me, though. The man who had run the cubs for years suddenly decided to leave, and he approached me to run it in his place. I had no experience of the Scouting Movement, and didn't much like what I saw . But he pointed out that I used to be a teacher, and I knew a lot of the boys, so I reluctantly agreed to do it for at least a year. I made three conditions: One, no religion, no church parades, no prayers after meetings. I did not agree with shoving Christianity down youngsters throats, and wanted no part in it. Two, no kit inspection, and Three, no drill. Both these smacked too much of quasi-military activities, like the Hitler Youth. To my surprise, all three were agreed to. So started as the Leader. I had an assistant, the mother of one of the cubs, who turned out to be great fun, and went along with all my ideas, such as they were.

After the first evening, I was confronted by a group of cubs with a request. Please could we have the inspections back, and please could we do drill sometimes? They were so young and earnest I gave in. After all, you could be safely militaristic at the age of eight, as long as you got over it later when you grew up to be twelve. I had played endless war games with my friend Sid at that age, and had it done me any harm? How could I know. It might have done Sid some harm, as he always had to be the German, and surely that might have left a mark. So we had inspections and drill after that, but not too much of either. It took me back to my time as Sergeant of Number One Platoon at Clayesmore, when I played at soldiers with real uniforms and real guns. I grew out of it, though, and avoided National Service like the plague.

We did Badges in the cubs, All the literature was supplied by the Scouting Movement, and very good it was. The cubs loved collecting badges, and we loved finding odd ways of doing things that would justify giving the badge. Swimming was easy, we borrowed a pool in one of the houses in Great Alne, owned by a parent. We did cooking by having a fire and roasting bacon and dough on sticks, as well as marshmallows and potatoes. We did map reading, and I fell out with Maggie my assistant, because I failed several cubs. She complained afterwards,

"You can't fail the poor little souls! They'll get miserable and stop enjoying things."

"That's Life, Maggie. You devalue the award if everyone passes. What's the point of doing well and passing, if every dunce can do it? Where's the sense of achievement? There has to be competition, and some must fail. They can succeed in other things, can't they? Life is not all about map reading!"

But I knew she had a point, so I gave the Failures another test, and made sure that they all passed, so honour was satisfied all round. In Life, everyone has Badges, eventually, but to get yours first time is a mark of honour. Not a bad motto for Living.

Maggie and I went to visit other cub packs, to get ideas. We found none, but we did find some horrific examples of dictatorship and excessive discipline. One run by two elderly ladies will stick in my mind for ever. The poor little cubs were not permitted to run about, nor speak unless spoken to. They never smiled, but lined up repeatedly to play their 'games', most of which seemed to be versions of what is done in a gym class. We did not stay to talk to the two harpies afterwards. They were both spinsters, and would have graced the SS in its heyday.

The Scouting Movement was full of oddballs, weirdoes and creeps. Some came to visit us, clearly suspicious of our 'No Religion' stance. One stuck his left hand out to greet me, saying when I stuck my right hand out, "Oh, you haven't been a Scout for long, have you, Mr. Bayley!"

"No, and I haven't been a creepy geek all my life either, like you have." I didn't say it, though. It would have got back to the Great Akela in the Sky, and I would have been in disgrace with my son.

We ran a football team on a Saturday, playing other cub packs in the area, but we didn't have enough for a full team. My daughter was a tomboy, and very keen on Peter Bonnetti, the goalkeeper for Chelsea. She had the full strip, boots and all, so we asked her to play in goal for the cubs. She was very good at it, until the sad day came when we had enough boys to make a team of eleven, and she had to step down. The boy who took her place was nearly useless, and she knew it. I think having to give up her goalie's place to an incompetent male marked her for life. It may have been the first time it happened, but it surely was not the last. It almost made her a violent Feminist on the spot, but her mother persuaded her not to sabotage the next match. They lost ten-nil, so she didn't need to anyway. Her brother thought it showed the dangers of letting Women into areas they had no business being in. He had a point there.

I did the full year that I had promised, and decided there were too many childish adults in the Scouting Movement for my liking, so I gave in my notice. Maggie was going off to college, my son and his friend were cooling in their interest in cubs, and there was a candidate to take over from me. So Tony became Leader. He was very enthusiastic, and bought some fibreglass canoes with the money we had raised at the Giant Barbecue. He lost the lot in one evening, and they were swept away down the River Alne, presumably to be recovered by some grateful people downstream, who thought their prayers had been answered. I think one was recovered by the cubs, on the bottom of the Avon, but the others disappeared for ever. Well done, Tony, the most incompetent Akela the village had seen. But I understand the kids had fun, which is the essential thing. Apart from not drowning the little dears, I suppose,Tony must have been lucky there. Perhaps it was all the swimming badges they had got under my charge.

In the History of Youth Clubs, the Scouting Movement comes near to the first youth organisations in the country, second only to Boys' Clubs and the YMCA. So in joining as the Akela of Great Alne Cubs, this was my first step in the direction of my life in youth clubs, although it didn't seem probable at the time. Also, middle age was creeping up on me. In my own classification, youth is 0 – 30. middle age is 30 – 60, old age is 60 – 90, and above that is Ancient. So now I was well over thirty, but not really aware of it. I had been through my transformation process of the beach at Littlehampton, and middle age didn't feel so much different from being young, although I knew surprises were in store.

My children were no longer little. They were growing up to be different beings from their parents, which was what we expected. Soon our oldest was at her Secondary school, with Big Ones. This was also where my wife taught, and my son was to go as well. Neither of them ever acknowledged their mother in the school corridors, and she ignored them too. It was the best way for all of them. My wife had come across some dire examples of teenage rebellion, and as she taught RE, this was quite severe at times. Many an evening she was despondent about going back next day, and I offered to let her give up and go back to Junior schools which she was trained for, but she always refused. The staff she worked with were supportive, as they all had the same problems, and the school was not in the least like St. Stephen's. Having my own kids there did mean that the conversation over the supper table was a bit limited for me and my youngest, at least. Discussion in depth of the school dinner menu and the dreariness of the lessons, as well as picking all the teachers to pieces, meant I was left twiddling my thumbs, unable to contribute anything to the conversation. Nobody wanted to hear about my dull days, and they were too young to listen appreciatively to my philosophies of Work, God and Why We Are Here.

Some of what they said was very funny. The placard announcing the school dinner menu was one of those where the letters could be picked off and placed differently. The dinner ladies were often upset when their careful notice of 'Jam tarts' became 'Jam Farts', especially when they were with 'bastard'. 'Mince' became 'Minge', and you can guess what became of 'rissoles'. It provided an endless source of fun for everyone except the dinner ladies. I suspected some of the staff did the more ingenious ones, but I could never prove it. There were some very naughty kids indeed there, but being a country school, there was never any really evil malice. The kids just offered the usual resistance to an educational syllabus designed by academic elite with no idea of how Real People thought and behaved. But in those days there were plenty of jobs, and even if you left with no qualifications, someone would employ you, even if it was working on the local nurseries, weeding and planting out seedlings. The girls always had the option of getting pregnant, and settling down in a council flat with their bloke, who usually turned out to be not too bad. There was, and is, a strong work ethic in the Town, and layabouts were barely tolerated. Crime was of the low-level kind, vandalism, punch-ups after closing time, shoplifting, taking cars and driving about at night, nothing major. Burglaries were mostly done by criminals coming in from Coventry or Birmingham, with the occasional local psychopath, who was always caught.

About this time, I took another job in the evenings. Word had got around that the local Open Borstal, Hewell Grange, were looking for people to run evening classes, and the pay was very good. So I applied, to find only two were vacant, Chess and Drama. Having done a little bit of amateur dramatics, I took on Drama. I was also doing a night class at Cannon Hill in Birmingham after work, on Documentary Drama, and I thought I could use what I learned in the class at Hewell Grange. So it proved.

My first evening there, I had a word with one of the Assistant Governors. He was a most educated and liberal man, and we talked about the value of drama in boosting self-confidence in inadequate people, and how he did not expect me to put on little plays for the entertainment of the other inmates, but he did want me to interact with them. This I was very willing to do, so I was eager to start when I walked into the room where the Lads were assembled, waiting for me to begin.

There was an utter silence. I wished them 'good evening', and got a faint mumble back. They just stared at me, waiting to see what I would do. I had been told that they were all from London, as the policy was to put them in a Borstal well away from their friends and relations. I told them a bit about myself, which got no response except some muffled laughter. Just like teenagers at my old Secondary Modern, I thought, except they were all over seventeen years old, and some were almost twenty, and large with it. I had discussed with my tutor in Cannon Hill how to break the ice, and at his suggestion, I started with some jokes, then invited them to tell me some. They did. They were some of the most disgusting and foul 'jokes' I had ever heard, but I knew they were testing me, to see if I would be shocked into telling them off. I knew better than that. This was not a school, so we continued. gradually, their jokes became funny, and they started laughing, and competing to get in the queue. I knew I had cracked it, and passed their test. I didn't blame them, they didn't want to be here, and certainly would reject any suggestion that this was to be like the schools that had failed to engage them back in London.

My tutor in Cannon Hill was most interested and helpful, and I don't know if I could have done it without his help. He even offered to come down with me one night, but I refused, thinking he would look so much better than I was that my status might be threatened. The Lads unbent a lot, and wanted to tell me their stories of why they were there, but I would not listen to them. I said I was interested in them as they were here, who they were now, and how they reacted to the Borstal situation. So we did some re-enactments of what had happened to them, and soon it became clear that they wanted to put on a play telling all their stories. The outline was first the Crime, a robbery with violence, and some interaction with another gang. Then the Arrest by the Police, then the Court Trial. They were terrific at improvising all the right words they must have heard so often.

:How do you plead, guilty or not guilty?'

"Not guilty, your Honour."

"Do you have anyone to represent you here in court?"

"No, your Honour."

"Then you may choose a representative. Do you see anyone you would want to represent you?"

"Yes, your Honour. That lady over there."

They told me that women lawyers always tried harder and worked longer hours on their cases, that's why they picked them if they could. The court scene was by far the longest, with shouting relatives swearing revenge on the witnesses, and the legal language was always spot-on accurate.

We never got beyond the court scene, because they were always found guilty, and the next scene would presumably take place exactly where we were, in custodial premises. We all knew about that, so the final scene was the Release, with sobbing mothers and girlfriends (in imagination only, none of them would act a woman, it was felt to be demeaning. The lady barristers were replaced by men soon into the trial, for the same reason)

We did other things besides this Great Drama, like improvising dialogues between people. It surprised me how they despised their victims, and disliked playing the part of one. They told me that the victims of their crimes were wimps, and deserved to be 'taken'. They had no insight whatsoever into what it might feel like to be a victim, since they had never been one. When they were beaten up or robbed in role-play, their immediate instinct was for revenge. They had no empathy at all for anyone who was not in their gang. This must be typical of criminals, as it certainly is of psychopaths. Many of them told me that they would do their 'bird' keeping their heads down, not getting into any trouble, and when they got out they would go straight back to crime. Many came from criminal families, and had been brought up knowing they would spend some of their time in prison. They did not resent this, it was just how their life was. The main aim was not to get caught, but none of them knew of anyone who was a criminal who had never done time. Even if there was no evidence, the police would make some up, and get them put away. They did not resent this either, they said they deserved it for all the crimes that had not been punished for. It was a like huge game to them, and they wanted to play it better. They used to teach each other the tricks of their chosen trade, so they came out better educated in crime than when they went in.

In my drama group there were a couple of boys who did not fit this pattern. They had been sentenced usually by a vindictive magistrate, often for a first offence, as an example to the community. These lads were a sorry sight, they were barely tolerated by the other career criminals, and they were used as lackeys, which role they accepted meekly, for a quiet life. They had not the spirit to resist, and if they did they were bullied. I do not know what became of them when they left, they had had whatever nerve they had possessed knocked out of them, and how they coped I do not know. They would be the ones taking the part of a woman in the role-play, because the others told them to.

I took them to the theatre twice. A neighbour of mine was a Probation Officer at Long Lartin, the maximum security prison nearby. It was his suggestion to take them, as he could come with me and provide extra help. The assistant governor was most enthusiastic, so Reg and I took about fifteen of them to Cannon Hill, to see The Threepenny Opera, by Kurt Weil and Berthold Brecht. At first, the lads were a bit anxious, as they had to wear their navy battle dress tops. The seats were near the front, since the production was in the round, but once the opera started, they forgot about being conspicuous, and got involved in the plot. It was very suitable, being about criminals, and Mack the Knife went down well with them. At the interval, we went to get a cup of coffee for each of them, and they became worried again, about being noticed. They formed a very tight group in one corner, with defensive/aggressive expressions on their faces, like a pack of Jack Russell dogs. Then to my dismay, an equally large group of hippies came in, with caftans, beads, long hair, and all the gear that was fashionable in the early 70s. They paused, seeing my lads, and there was a long freeze. My heart was racing, it was like some cowboy film where the baddies meet the goodies, before the fight begins. After what seemed like an hour, the hippies moved on, and my lads relaxed. They eyed each other up from time to time, but there was no action. The lads never even mentioned it afterwards.

The second theatrical trip was not so well liked. We went to see "Zigger Zagger" at the Alex, and the set consisted of a football stand on-stage. It was a young group of actors putting on the production, and after a brief introduction, they came out into the audience, looking for people to come up on stage and be the football crowd. My lads were aghast. They felt conspicuous enough sitting in their seats in their blue tops, but to go on stage, and have a luvvie ask them why they were wearing it, in front of all that audience... their worst nightmare come true. They sank down in their seats trying not to be noticed, but the actor got closer and closer. He looked at them, and if looks could kill, he would have dropped lifeless on the spot, shrivelled up and totally dead. He got the message from all fifteen pairs of eyes. He passed on. The lads never recovered from that horrific moment. They made it very plain on the way back that I was never ever to ask them to go to the theatre again, if that was the risk they had to face. So I never did.

One evening, we were rehearsing the fight scene of our Great Epic. As it was rather chaotic, we were doing it in slow motion, which they enjoyed. All at once, the door burst open and two screws (warders) burst into the room, and started laying about them, pulling lads apart and shouting. Immediately, everyone froze. The screws were baffled. "What's going on here, then?" one asked in an aggressive way. I did my best to explain, but they were plainly annoyed, as their image had been damaged, they had made fools of themselves. We did our best to laugh it off, and went on, but none of our hearts were in it.

I got a message to see the Assistant Governor at the end of the session. He sat me down, and explained that two cultures existed side by side in Hewell Grange. He and I were the liberal side, keen on education, the restorative powers of the arts, reformation not punishment. But the screws (he called them that) were of the opposite opinion. Prison was punishment, the inmates here were being treated far too well, etc. etc. He told me to do my best to avoid them, keep out of their way, as he gave me his full support, and what I was doing was exactly the right thing. But he could have little power over the screws, who were union dominated and had a narrow view of right and wrong. He said that by and large, the inmates agreed with the screws, but that we liberals were able to be intelligent about what we did, and not force any confrontation. The whole incident encapsulated perfectly the two attitudes I had found in schools as well. I understood him very well, and promised to be careful.

They actually offered me a job there, full time, three days and two evenings a week. The pay would have been better than I was getting at Lusac, but I had to turn it down. I could not face working inside a prison for too many hours a week, it would depress me. And the continuous battle between the screws and the liberals was not an easy one to fight, as I had found in St. Stephen's rotten little prison of a school.

After Christmas, I went back to find that four of my class had absconded, going back home to London. They were picked up easily, and they were then sent to a regular Borstal, so I never saw them again. I had some new pupils, but they only wanted to muck about. I struggled until Easter, then I put it to the group. Do you want to do it my way, or not? If not, I was leaving. It was a narrow vote, but they voted for me to go, so I went. I had had my fun, after all, and really enjoyed it when it went well. I often wonder if I helped to give those four lads sufficient confidence to abscond, hoping to blag their way past police looking for them. I hope I did, in a way.

STEP FOUR --GAINING HEIGHT

THE WORLD OF CRETINUS BOREDOM

Cretinus Boredom rolled over in his bed and switched off the alarm buzzer. He was aware that he had completed his assignments from the previous day, and he was ready for yet more at the Sixth Form College. He got out of bed and carefully chose his T-shirt for the day, which declared him to be "F***ing for Freedom" in bright red letters. If only, he thought.

His parents were already at breakfast, looking harassed, for their days were not so carefree as those of their only child, Cretinus. His name was not actually 'Cretinus Boredom', it was Cedric Bolden, but the nickname had been given him by the boys at his school, and it had stuck. He didn't mind much, it gave him street-cred of a kind. He ate his processed wheat flakes in silence, going over his day as he watched morning TV.

There was Civics first, compulsory in every course now, in which he took meticulous notes, hoping to get an A Grade. Then English Literature, where they were studying the novels of Iris Murdoch, one of which he had in his briefcase, with the essay he had written on 'Her Place in Modern Literature'. Next was Business Studies, where they were going over the role of Government Agencies in the Economy. He was in the middle of his coursework, and later in the day he would go down to the Council Offices to see the Officer for Tourism and Rural Redevelopment to ask what he did. He had a thick report to read on it before he went.

After lunch, he would study in the IT room for his Computer Studies course, as he had an essay to write on "The Internet -- its place in the National Economy". Then a lecture in the Economics department, probably to do with Community Potentials for Funding Assignations. They had fallen behind on the new syllabus and had several essays to catch up.

He muttered his farewells to his parents as they ferreted nervously about, looking for things misplaced since they stopped work exhausted at ten the previous night. His mother was a teacher, who was always surrounded by a miasma of anxiety and a mound of marking. His father was a middle manager in an accountancy firm, and he worked long hours in the office, and brought home a lot of work at weekends. He hardly knew his parents now, but it didn't seem to matter, as he was very busy himself. Weekends meant time at the gym, long fitness runs in the grey streets to keep in trim, and much reading to keep up to date in his studies.

He walked to college, and went at a good pace, feeling his muscles stretch and strain as his feet hit the grey pavement. He noticed the headlines at the paper-shop, "Crime figures up", but he never had time to read papers. In his head he went over the essay he had written the previous night, "Crime and the Law" for his Civics course, and recalled that he had postulated that crime would one day be eradicated by the rigourous implementation of Criminal Laws, and he wondered if he was correct in his assumptions. He remembered that he had to give a talk tonight at the Young Liberals, thanking them for the support they had given him, in the form of a cheque for £5.75, for his part in writing the new Local Government Manifesto.

He was just wondering whether to make some comic reference to the Tories or not, when he was knocked violently aside by a young man. Then he was smashed in the face by a fist, and he heard a voice screaming "Give us yer money." He fell to the pavement, and his head banged; he was aware of the two muggers laughing, then all went black.

When he awoke, he was sitting against a shop front. There was no-one around, and people were hurrying past. Surely they must see that I am hurt, thought Cretinus, but they continued to ignore his feeble attempts to attract their attention. They think I am just another drunk, or a druggie, he thought. If only they realised who I am....

Well, who am I? The thought shot through his mind like a lightning stab. I'm Boredom, that's who I am. My life is one long essay on meaning, yet it has no meaning of its own.

None at all. Who am I? That's a good question, I must try and think about it.

The more he tried to think, the more he became confused. What do I do? I write essays, do assignments, read documents, books, but why? He realised he had a new feeling, one he recalled from childhood. Excitement. It was making his heart beat, his mind race. He hadn't felt this for....years now. Why now? It must be the bang on his head. Then he thought, no. It was those two thugs. They were laughing as they approached, and when they ran away. It had been years since he laughed himself. The best years of his life, they said. And he never laughed. He just worked. Why? To get a good job. Like his parents? Did they laugh?

A strange emotion flooded into his whole mind and body, and took away his breath suddenly. It was time to...do something. He stared at the shop window, and picked up a large stone. He looked up and down the street, and then threw it hard at the window.

You will now be aware that all the steps are in place to Start A Youth Club. So far, I had never set foot inside one, nor had any inclination so to do. I was not aware of a youth-club-shaped hole in my life, no blinding vision had dazzled me with a voice crying "Bill! You must go forth and set up a youth club, so that your Soul may be Enlightened, for so it is written! Alleluia!" I vaguely knew of the existence of one in

Elcaster, but I didn't know what it did, nor who ran it, nor which kids went to it. I just assumed that there was one, every Town had one, and Elcaster was no different. I knew it wasn't anywhere near me, as I assumed it would be a nuisance, with kids making a racket, committing vandalism, getting stroppy and rude outside it. I didn't read anything about the achievements of Elcaster's superb youth club, but neither did I read about how much disapproval it engendered with the Good People of the Town. I asked my own kids if they knew of one, and they just shrugged. They were at the age when that answer came for almost every question, except "Do you want any more money?", so I thought nothing of it. My wife thought there was one, as her Bad Boys sometimes talked about it, and what happened there, and who went, and especially which girls were there, but she didn't know any details. She would not have gone within half a mile of it if she had known about it, because it presumably had as its members all the troublesome kids she struggled with on a daily basis.

I was reaching yet another Crisis Point in my life. The job at Lusac was so boring and precarious that I was seriously thinking of what to do next. My Career Concept was lying wounded on the floor of my subconscious, but it had not yet expired, and the dangers of being without a job at all seemed to revive it. Furthermore, my kids were getting older. To other people, this might not have mattered, but to me it was a potential loss. They no longer needed my company in the evenings, except as a bugbear that my wife used to frighten them with. "Get that cleared up/ mend that/ fix that/ stop fighting/behave yourselves BEFORE YOUR FATHER GETS HOME!." They usually did, and I was unaware of the contortions and dramas enacted as I drove home from Birmingham. Peace usually reigned as I stepped in the door. The scars inflicted on the plaster, the walls, the doors, were not seen by me, and had to be pointed out years later by my kids, who knew that by then I could do nothing. After all, by then they were in their thirties. I found it funny when they described the furious fights they got into, what was thrown, how they distracted me. I don't suppose I would have found it funny at the time. My poor wife certainly did not.

We had moved house by this time, to a Grade 2 listed building in the Town, 350 years old, and half-timbered. It had four bedrooms, which was the main point in moving from our three-bedroom semi on the outskirts. We also felt that we were not going to move from Elcaster, and we wanted to be more a part of the Town, nearer the Centre of Action, if there was such a place. It was a corner shop when we bought it, but the business was valued at zero. The owner told us she had been working for seventy hours for twenty pounds profit, and when VAT came in, that was her last straw. We put our semi up for sale, and made an offer on the old shop. Our semi was sold in two days, to a friend, who didn't understand how houses are bought and sold, and thought he had to go to the Estate Agent instead of coming to me with his offer. The Agent amiably agreed to lower his fees, and we began the anxious wait for a mortgage. It came eventually, not before the old shop seller had tried to sell to another buyer, but our agent persuaded her to stick with us. When I went to settle up with the agent, the boss, a Mr. Such, dealt with me. I noticed he had charged me full price for selling my own house.

"Your agent promised us a reduction, due to you having to do no work at all."

"Yes, but business is business. Sorry."

"Well, Mr. Such, you are not an Elcaster man, and you don't keep your word. I shall make sure everyone in Elcaster knows what a scoundrel you are."

He smiled wanly. He knew what I did not; that the whole of Elcaster thought him a scoundrel with no morals, but that's estate agents, isn't it? So what?

We moved in like an African family moves house, using a friendly builder's truck piled high with furniture and rubbish, with the kids riding in the back waving to all their friends as we trundled the mile down the road to our new home on the corner. We celebrated our new home with some friends, drinking her home-made beer, and finding we were hopelessly drunk after an hour. It was the first of a series of great housewarming parties we had there. We disposed of all the stock of the shop, the sweets disappearing into the kids' bedrooms in the twinkling of three pairs of greedy little eyes. We smoked the rolling tobacco, drank the fizzy drinks, gave the dog food to the cat, saved the old birthday cards for future use. Many of our friends got used to cards wishing them a Happy Third Birthday, with a nought scrawled in, if they were actually thirty. The joke wore a bit thin after ten years, but we still have those cards put away somewhere. We used the Syrup of Figs somehow, and the boot-polish, and the cereals, not to mention the shoelaces, the kirby-grips, hair nets, and nail varnish. It all went somewhere. There was not much, as the poor lady had let the stock run down for a long time before she decided to sell. We used the bacon counter for a guinea-pig cage (they all died later), the old ice-cream fridge as a freezer, the marble tops as a window ledge and a new table. The steel shelves we spread around the house and the garage. We kept the old-fashioned bacon slicer, until one of our kids played with it nearly slicing her fingers off, when we put it away on a cupboard. We still have it, it will be an antique soon. We got used to the noise of the traffic in about two nights. My youngest was caught throwing conkers down on passing children, who threw them back, and resented, quite rightly, being told off about it. "She threw it first!" was their plaintive cry.

It was good to be able to watch people pass right by our windows, as we had no front garden, the front wall being right on the pavement. There was a downside to this, which I will explain later, as it led indirectly to my going to a youth club. (At last!). The garden was appalling, just a dump of mud, so I got some turf and some earth and made a hasty garden where we could sit in the sun. We tried an archaeological dig in the muddy 'lawn', until an expert told us that the Roman layer was nine feet down. I did not fancy digging with my kids at that depth, so we filled it in, leaving the treasures behind for later generations. I ripped out the ugly tiled fireplace, hoping to find a lovely old fireplace behind it, only to discover nothing but a gaping hole. I built a temporary fireplace out of bricks I found in the garden, with a wooden surround given me by my father-in-law. It is still there, waiting for me to build a fancy one, thirty-eight years after.

We did not put the furniture in place straight away. I left three rooms completely empty, and hung a lot of pictures on the walls, that I had framed in the interval waiting for the sale to go through. I sent invitations to everyone I could think of, and waited for the cash to roll in. And it did, unbelievably. After a week, I had sold three-quarters of the paintings, and we had a party after the last day, the like of which we had never had before. It went on until seven in the morning, and later it was to be the indirect cause of at least two marriages breaking up. I put the furniture in, and settled down to see what I was going to do.

I did nothing. I had to work, of course, and that had got duller with each passing month. I sat and looked at the house, wondering what changes I might make. The old shop looked a mess, all the shelves taken away left the walls looking shabby. I did not want start work on the house until I had got a feel for it. It was older than any house we had lived in, and must have a character that would reveal itself in time. First impressions were not all that good. There was a lot of timber showing on the outside, but almost none on the inside, which meant it was covered up with plaster. There were only two beams in the whole of the inside, and I knew there must be many more. My solicitor thought I was reckless not to have had my own survey done.

"What if there's woodworm?" he asked, as if he alone had thought of it.

"Of course there's woodworm, lots of it. But the beams are so big and old that the woodworm gives up after penetrating a couple of inches. What's that in a beam that's over a foot square?" He still thought I was nuts. We had had to promise to have the roof done as a condition of getting the mortgage, but I was in no hurry. Let the house speak to me before rushing around changing things you later regret.

I waited nearly eighteen months before I stated. The mortgage people were getting ratty, so I found a local builder to replace all the faulty tiles. When he had done that, I began by removing plaster in the old shop, revealing beams galore, then patching up the plaster around the beams. It looked great, so I did the same in the other downstairs rooms. I took all the hardboard off the walls, and the doors, and got a mate of mine to replaster the living room.

"I'm not very good, Bill," he said. "I can't get the walls even."

"Just look at the place, Bob. No wall in the whole place is even. I want wobbly plaster. It's in the character of the place. Just make sure it's waterproof."

We had to put in a damp course, by injection of silicone

into the walls. We tried to get a grant to do some of the work. The council sent an idiot round to look.

"You'll have to raise the ceiling above the stairs, and put in bigger windows. Then you need cavity walls throughout."

I pointed out that it was a listed building, and I wouldn't be allowed to do any of that. Besides, why put in a cavity wall, thus destroying the bare beam effect? "This room only has less than ten percent of its walls in contact with the outside. How much heat do you think it will lose that way?"

Either the man was an incompetent ass, or he was just going through the motions to prevent us applying for a grant. Whichever, probably both, we did not apply.

I stripped all the old paint off the doors, once the hardboard's removal had revealed panelled wooden doors. I used a blowtorch and a stripping knife. I ruined the first side I tried, covering it with little burn marks, but the second went well, and I did all of them. They looked good. I was getting the feel of the place now. It was a jerry-built house when put up three-and-a-half centuries ago, probably for farm workers. There had been five cottages in a row, with a single room downstairs, a scullery, and probably two bedrooms. Some time in the Victorian period, the end two must have deteriorated so much that they were demolished, and houses built on the site. Of the other three, I had two, which meant I had two front doors, and two back doors as well. Ripe for a French farce. There had been additions, and additions to the additions, but the old plan was still there.

Nobody had ever had enough money to really do the place up, my predecessors were all like me, enough money to improve the old house, but not enough to change it radically, like some of the big houses further up the street. Consequently, the houses in our street were a total hotchpotch of ages, from the 1300s up to the 1960s. Ours was somewhere in the middle. It was no beauty, nor of any great architectural interest, but it felt comfortable and welcoming. It suited us perfectly. It felt as if it had been a home to many families, and had been loved, if a bit neglected. I was glad to be the latest in a long line of owners. There had probably been houses on our site right back to Roman times, or before, since the archaeologists had found the Roman wall went a few metres North of our house, next to the River Arrow. The old bridge must have been there in one form or another for centuries, and was probably a ford before becoming a bridge. The Forest of Arden would have begun on the opposite river bank to us, with its wolves, boars, bears and dark mystery. Sometimes I can see it clearly in my mind, and it gives me comfort to think someone like me has been sitting here and looking across the river for over 2000 years. I am merely the latest, and I hope not to be the last.

During the initial stages of accustoming ourselves to our new house, some of the drawbacks became apparent. It was cold, so we had central heating put it. The poor man who installed it broke three chisels, two saws and a screwdriver in trying to cut notches in the oak beams holding up the floor. I had asked him to look out for any that needed replacing.

After a week of sweating, he glared balefully at me when I asked about it. "Replacing? It's going to be me that needs replacing. That old oak is like cast iron. Look!", and he showed me a lump of dark brown stuff that certainly looked like iron. "There's not a trace of any grain in that! I can't prise it apart. I'm having to grind the notches with an electric drill!" I was reassured about the durability of our old place, even if he was delayed by the toughness of the wood.

After about three months one of the main troubles with the house became obvious. It was built right on the pavement, no front garden or any space at all. Normally, this was fine, but the trouble came on a Friday or a Saturday night, after closing time in the pubs. We were on the rat-run for the drunks going home. The working man and his family lived in the main across the river, on the Canway Estate, built in the 1950s. There were no pubs on it, probably because of the temperance mindset of the local bigwigs refusing planning permission. So on a Friday and a Saturday, the working men liked to patronise some of the local hostelries, of which there were quite a lot. They liked to stay there and drink as long as possible. Then they would wend their merry way home past our house. Our house was on the corner before the bridge, the last one you would pass when going home to the Canway. So if you wanted to make something of a mark in the Town, our house was your last chance. And many of them took it, rapping on the windows, shouting in the street, sometimes fighting, talking loudly, falling against the walls or the doors, pissing in the doorways, carrying their comatose mates home, and generally being loud, at midnight and after. I was not too fussed, I liked a drink myself, but my wife found it threatening, and so the kids got worried too. There was nothing we could do about it, though. Probably people had been sitting where we were on Friday nights (or whatever the Latin for Friday is), and moaning about the drunks going past, or stopping to argue. So we were only the latest to suffer. Too bad.

In fact, the adults were at least predictable, and I knew one or two of them from meeting them in the pubs. There were a lot of pubs, for a small town. There was the Red Horse, The Hollybush, the Town Hall, the Turks Head, The Bear, The Oak, The Cross Keys, The Swan, The Crown, The Bell, The White Lion, The Dog and Partridge, the Conservative Club, The Nelson, the White Hart, all within walking distance of each other. The only drinking place North of the river Arrow was the Trades and Labour Club, yet most of the Town's pub-going population lay North of the river, which meant we got a lot of the walking traffic, not to mention staggering, stumbling, weaving, chasing, running, singing, knocking, shouting and quarrelling traffic. But only on a Friday, or a Saturday.

But their kids used our corner too. Knocking and running is still an Olympic-style sport in Elcaster, and we got quite a lot. There were three ways to run after you had knocked at our front door. Up the street, down across the bridge, or round the corner into School Road. And each escape route had other branches off it, so catching them was a problem. They knew that too, which made us a target.

I knew enough not to go out and rant every time. This would make the sport much more fun, and would encourage all and sundry to do it. Even the adults did it, but only after closing time. I was amazed to find how many thirty or forty year-olds would knock at my door in the early hours, as if they were reliving their childhood, reminding themselves of the fun they had had as kids. But the kids were a bit of a nuisance, because I didn't know any of them They knew my wife, of course, and they knew where she lived, which probably made things marginally worse. But it was always me that had to respond in some way to their irritations. It was not sensible to ignore it either. That made them try harder. There was a middle point where my response would lessen their annoying habits, but only minimise them. It would never eliminate them, I knew that. It was a tradition of the Town, and who was I to try to stop it? I had to take my part in the tradition, and do the best I could.

Readers who have persevered up to this point will be wondering if I ever did get to a youth club. I can understand the frustration you must be feeling, but never fear! Takeoff is at hand! All the years of preparation have been completed, all the social norms are in place, and my public duty antennae were twitching. It would be good to say that was how I felt at the time, but it was not. It took a phone call to galvanise me into my orbit of community service, if that is what you call it.

The phone call came from a friend of mine, Chris Gough (later to be called into service for the community as the Mayor of Elcaster, not once, but several times. I have lost count of how many, and so has he). He knew I used to be a teacher, so he asked me a very simple question. Would I consider going as a volunteer to the local youth club, because they were running out of adults to help there. Chris himself was on the management committee of the club, but did not want to actually get involved with teenagers himself. How many times have I heard that from grown men, who could do the job very well if only they had the nerve? No, that is not right. It's not nerve they lack. They lack nothing, in fact. They have an abundance of common sense, and they know better than to get working with a bunch of tearaway hooligans, for no money or thanks. But I digress.

I promised him I would think about it, little knowing how much danger I was in, teetering upon the edge of a morass, the like of which I could not imagine. I discussed it with my wife, who thought it might be quite a good idea, as long as I didn't expect her to join in. Of course I did not. She had already told me by this time that I would be the very last person on earth that she would ever work with. She did not seem to think that bringing up three kids, two dogs and a cat was work, which I did, but I kept quiet. We had been married about fifteen years by this time, so the first blush was gone from our union, but we were still together, and still fighting, each other as well as the Problems of Life, you understand.

I can recall my thinking as if it were yesterday. I was not busy in the evenings, as my painting only took place after ten at night, when the kids were in bed, and I could be sure I would not be interrupted by annoying phone calls and friends coming round to ask me out for a drink. I had experience with such teenagers, and my wife knew a lot of them, so could fill me in on the really awkward ones, even if she declined to get involved. But two things clinched it for me. First my kids were getting older, my eldest was around fifteen, and had no real use for me as a companion any more. So if I couldn't play with my own kids, I would find ones kicking around on the streets to borrow, and a youth club was the ideal place to find them. The second reason was that I would get to know the scrotes who knocked on my window, and they would not be frightening to me any more. Fear comes from the unknown, and once you know your enemy, you are no longer frightened of him.

So I rang Chris back later in the week and said I would turn up at his youth club when it next met, and see what happened. I was making no promises, mind. He was pleased, and told me it was on a Tuesday at the Grogg Hall, in a hut behind the main building. I knew little about the Grogg Hall, except that it put on dances and quizzes, and my daughters had learned ballet there for about a month before getting bored, and that the local Amateur Dramatic Society and the Operatics Society put on plays and musicals on their stage.

My youngest went to the Red Cross there, to learn to be a nurse, or whatever it was they did. The name of the leader was Jim, and he was a tax inspector by trade. My heart sank a little, and I imagined a stern humourless man like an accountant, and I wondered if I would get on with him. Chris said he was a volunteer, as the County Youth Service declined to send anyone to work there, for various political reasons he didn't want to go into at this time. I learned them later, in Spades.

So the next Tuesday I took myself along to the hut behind the Grogg, at seven thirty, and opened the door. I was not prepared for what greeted me. Remember, I had never set foot in a youth club before in my life. The noise! It was pandemonium in there, and I could only see about ten kids, who were racketing around shrieking at the tops of their voices. Some were banging table-tennis bats against the table with a sound like gunfire, others were just jumping in the air and landing with a thump, and all were just making a colossal din. I looked for an adult, any adult. I saw a man on the other side of the room, reading some notes and oblivious to the noise. I walked over and introduced myself. "Bill Bayley, you must be Jim. Did Chris tell you I was coming?."

He looked a very pleasant man, and he shook my hand. "Yes, he did tell me. Sorry about the noise," he said in a loud voice that I could hardly hear above the din, "but we allow them to let off steam when they first come in, it saves trouble in the long run. They'll calm down in a minute. I'll introduce you to them."

And so they did, and so he did. They seemed all right, a bit out of breath, but they shook my hand politely enough. "Let's get the table-tennis league going, " said Jim, and they set up the net, and started playing really very expertly. "The other adults will be here in a bit, there's three of them. Big Abe, Wally and Margaret. Margaret does the food, well, tea and coffee, and doesn't have a lot to do with the kids. The other two do."

They all came in together. Big Abe was like huge hippy, with a beard and gappy teeth. He reminded me of an amiable shambling ape. I found it hard not to call him 'Big Ape' in my head, as this was bound to slip out, and doubtless offend him. Wally came in with his son, a surly lad who said nothing. Margaret was younger, only just married, with no kids, but wanting to get involved with the community somehow. She had just left the Army, and told me she was used to rough kids, and could answer back with the best of them. Wally and Big Abe were soon involved with the teenagers, and a row soon broke out between Abe and two fifteen-year-olds. Jim sorted it out. Big Abe was indignant with Jim. "You should have sent them home, Jim, they were really rude to me, insulting." Jim just nodded. Then Wally had an argument with his son, who left in a huff, with his father shouting after him, "There'll be no supper! I shall tell your mother!"

I don't remember much more about my first night in a

youth club. I do recall liking and respecting Jim as a man I could work with, especially as he sighed as Wally and Big Abe left. "Those two are more trouble than all the other kids put together, but we have to put up with them. Their hearts are in the right place. It's just that their brains are non-existent." I saw exactly what he meant. Marg was of a very different calibre. She watched and talked to the few girls that had come that night, and she knew a lot about them, who was related to who, who was going out with who, who had broken up with who. She lived locally, as I did, and she was invaluable to Jim, who lived miles away, and didn't know Elcaster at all.

So that was my first experience at a youth club. It was not revelatory, nor an apotheosis. I did not think. "At last! I have found my Purpose in Life! I know now what to do for the rest of my existence!" It made me tired, but not excessively so. It had given me some laughs, and I liked Jim and Marg, and thought I could get on with Big Abe and Wally. Jim was pleased to have me, a normal male who probably wouldn't start arguments with the kids that Jim had to sort out, and with some experience with teenagers, even if in school rather than in the wild. When Chris rang to ask how it went, I said I would certainly go back, and lend Jim a hand, and I might even get to like it in time. How innocent I was then!

I did go back every Tuesday for several years. I even got to enjoy it, in a slightly masochistic kind of way. I certainly found Jim a good person to work with, he was supportive when needed, had a good sense of humour and knew what could be ignored, he knew what had to be tackled there and then in case things got out of hand. It was no different from teaching, I realised, but without the threat of the headmaster, the parents, the school ethos, the exams, and so on. In fact it was not like a school except that it had kids in it. They had come mainly because it was not like school, and they could enjoy the company of their mates without all the social expectations that schools thrust upon their pupils. That's not to say we did not have expectations, though. We expected good manners towards the adults, and the Law of the Land had to be obeyed, so there was no fighting, no stealing, no murdering. No drink and no drugs. Trying to enforce 'no littering' was a complete waste of time. They threw stuff down as if the place was a littler bin. We used to attempt to get them to sweep up after it was finished, but they had the knack of disappearing just before we asked them to help, or they had an excuse so they had to be home at once. Usually it was the adults who swept up, and tidied things away. Nobody else used the hut, so we did not have to be too particular, and we could leave things out until next time if we wanted. The table-tennis table took up a lot of the space, and could remain where it was, as did the dart-board and the table football.

After a while, I wondered what brought them to the youth club in the first place, and why did they keep coming. My own kids would never have set foot over the threshold, the members were not the kids my own children wanted to mix with after school, although they mixed with them well enough in school. It was the old class thing, but translated into peer friendships. There was nothing unpleasant about it, it was a reflection of the adult's lives in Elcaster; some went to the Trades & Labour, some to the Grogg Hall bar or the Bell, and in Elcaster the twain hardly mixed at all. Nobody seemed to mind, that was just how it was.

So most of the kids we had as members came off the Canway Estate, and went to the High School where my wife taught, and two of my own kids went. Some of them were in other groups, but a lot were not. The youth club was the only organisation they belonged to outside school. They sniffed when asked why they weren't in the Scouts, or the Cadets. "They're too stuck up." was often the answer, and it meant that they felt they were not welcome at these other groups. They did not like the discipline expected of them there, either. They liked racketing around, and they would not be allowed to in any other group but ours.

They wanted to be with their mates, too, and interact with them. This did not always involve being friendly, and occasionally bitter feuds broke out, between individuals or between groups. Fighting was banned, but insults were hurled, rude signs generated, in fact everything that indicated aggression except physical violence. I soon realised that one of the main reasons they came was to meet adults who were not parents, teachers, relatives or officials. Adults who had no axe to grind with them, and had no expectations bar that they be polite, mostly. And of course, they pushed the boundaries of what 'polite' meant, all the time. One of their principle entertainments was to annoy the adults, sometimes in subtle ways, other times in direct confrontation. As an adult, it was up to you how you responded. I had seen that attitude in the classroom, so I knew not to let real anger show, but if you were annoyed, then show it by acting annoyed. Better still was to react with a smile, or a shrug. They would try it on with someone else then. Once they got to know your boundaries they mostly stopped testing them, although they had known Jim a long time, yet still tried his patience deliberately once in a while. They saw it as their duty, I think. They were teenagers, we were grown-ups, therefore they must annoy us, it was the way of things. I went along with that tradition myself, and did not object to it. But Big Abe and Wally never got used to it. The kids could wind up Big Abe in under a minute usually, unless he had chilled out on a spliff before he came, in which case he was more amiable. Wally was almost as bad, but did have the use of thoroughgoing stupidity to help him, often useful when dealing with relatively clever kids. They just give up when the stupid don't get their taunts, and go and tease a more intelligent adult, with the desired results. They hardly ever teased Margaret. I think it was because she never reacted the way they wanted, and she could see their taunting ways a mile off, and they knew it. They talked to her all right, especially the girls, but she never gossiped, so the girls knew they could tell her some quite confidential stuff, she would never pass it on. She would tell us a little when we were sweeping up, the things that had made her laugh, and we would swap stories of the events of that night, and previous nights, just like the old teachers had in my first school in Swindon.

We even went on some outings. We planned to take some one Sunday to the Malvern Hills. Walking was not one of the activities high on the 'to-do' list of our members, but about six put their names down, As well as Jim and I, we took Big Abe and Wally. We made our own lunches, and on the minibus, it was amazing to see the difference in size of the various people's luggage. Some had none, with their sandwiches in their pockets. One didn't even have any sandwiches, he said he would 'buy them up there'. We pointed out that there were no shops at all where we were going, and the amazement on his face was plain. He could not imagine any place without shops. Big Abe had a huge rucksack. "Oh yes, I'm an experienced rambler, I've got all the equipment in here for coffee, tea, you name it. You'll be glad of my foresight when we're up on British Camp in the wind!" He smugly settled in his seat while Jim drove us there.

Up on the Hills, the wind was strong, but it was not cold. Big Abe set off at a frantic pace, mocking the rest of us for being unfit. We plodded on up the path to the summit, whilst Big Abe cut across, taking the steepest route to the top. After a while, we noticed that Big Abe was no longer in sight. "Let him go," said Jim, "We're better off without him." He spoke too soon. Turning a corner, we saw Big Abe sitting disconsolately near the path, plainly exhausted. "Sorry chaps, " he gasped out. "My asthma has come on, I can't go any further." Jim persuaded him to walk with us, slowly, whilst we carried his huge rucksack, which weighed a ton. Jim muttered to me, "He doesn't have asthma. He's just not fit, and he's worn himself out by showing off." This was obviously true, so we carried his stuff with us the whole day. It also turned out that, far from having the equipment to make tea and coffee, it was mostly electronic stuff, so that Big Abe could listen to his cronky New Age music as he munched huge numbers of sandwiches, bread rolls, sausages, cakes, and other delicacies he needed for his day in the hills. He did manage to scoff the lot, so we didn't have to carry it back for him. Meanwhile, Wally had fallen out with his son, who had stormed off in a huff, and we did not know where he had gone. As he was an incredibly stupid boy, we had to go looking for him. We found him eventually, but he refused to walk with us and insisted on being 100 metres behind. Jim sighed to me, "I told you the volunteers were more trouble than the kids. Never again!"

Jim was a volunteer, and didn't get paid for his time, and nor did the rest of us. I asked one day why there was no County Youth Service in Elcaster. It was a long story, and it clearly annoyed Jim, but he told it to me. The Grogg Hall had been built in 1953 at a cost of £50,000 by a David Grogg, owner of the grocery chain, Groggs. It was built in memory of his wife, now dead, Hannah Susan Grogg, who had stayed in Elcaster during the War and was much taken with the kindness of the people. She thought they should have a place where the youth of the Town could go in the evenings, so when she died, David Grogg persuaded the Town Council to give some land, and the Hall was built. It was supposed to be a youth club, said Jim, but you only have to look at it to see it was never intended as that. It's a Town Dance and Banqueting Hall, and it's almost useless as a youth club. Too much glass, a sprung dance floor, much too good for a youth club. But it did open as one, with much Press coverage, and lots of equipment lying around to show the reporters, including a cine projector. The Youth Service said they should pay for a youth worker too, but they would not. By this time, old David Grogg was in a wheelchair, and was heard to say as they pushed him into the building in whose structure he had taken no interest , "This is not a Youth Club, it's a Dance Hall!"

How right he was. In three weeks, the youth club equipment had gone, back to where it had been borrowed from. The cine projector also disappeared, never having shown a single film. The youth club ran in the main hall, thanks to some dedicated volunteers, but it was plainly unsuited to the ravages of kids, and there were endless scraps between the youth club and the trustees. One lady volunteer was later a magistrate, one Mrs. Roman, and by all accounts she was brilliant. But even she had little clout when it came to keeping the youth club in the hall, so it moved to the hut, where it is at present.

The kids I met there were a very mixed bunch. They all went to the local High School, except those who were suspended, and there were none who went to the Grammar School. My own kids and their friends would never have become members. "It's a club for people who cannot join anything else", someone said. It was not that they could not join, it was more that they would not. They nosed out anything that smelled of moralising, or if they tried to promote 'Middle Class Values', as St. Stephen's put it. They had their own values, and very strong they were.

First, never grass on your mates, no matter what.
Second, be very cautious about everything new, especially if introduced to it by an adult.
Third, follow what your mates do, stick with them, then it's proven to be safe.
Fourth, do what's fashionable for teenagers, and spend as much money on it as you can get hold of, to impress others
Fifth, respect your family (except when you're talking to them in private) and get revenge on anyone who slags them off, especially your Mum.
Sixth, do your best to annoy any adult, but not too much if you respect them. (There were quite a few adults that they did respect, mainly the ones who treated them like adults, and who gave teenagers respect in their turn).

These values did not seem too bad to me, and I still think so. They usually gave respect when respect was given, and it didn't have to be by trying to be their friend, which as an adult you never could be. You had to try to see these kids as the adults of Elcaster of the future, which of course they were. I still see lots of them. Many are now grandparents, and it has always given me a great buzz to say to a kid. "You think you're trouble? You're not half as bad as your Mum (or Dad, or even Grandpa or Grandma) used to be when they came to this youth club." They often stop teasing you at this point, fearing that you might actually go round and talk about them to the former member, their Mum. Maybe it's out of respect for my age, but I doubt it.

"And why does the County provide nothing, no youth workers?" I asked Jim one night. He snorted. "Because they always say that the Grogg Hall was provided as a youth club and should provide its own youth worker, which it never will. The two Grogg trustees detest the youth club. They'd get rid of us at the drop of a hat if the could find some excuse. The County have sent one or two workers here, but they always fell out severely with the trustees and left. They won't touch it now, yet the Grogg is set up as a youth club in its Constitution. Ironic, isn't it?"

I thought it was more than ironic, it was downright unjust, and something should be done, like reporting them to the Grogg family for what they were failing to do. Jim just shrugged his shoulders, he was not a political kind of man. "That would do no good. David Grogg's nephew, Young Dennis Grogg, is a part-time trustee as well as a stockbroker in London, and he sanctions every decision the two trustees make, no questions asked. He doesn't care a jot about Elcaster. No, let's just leave it. We are here, we pay our rent, we have a good management committee that deals with the trustees and keeps both of them off our backs. Let it go, Bill. We're doing all right." And at that time, I believed that he was correct.

My presence in the Elcaster youth club was noted by a youth worker who was placed at the Stratford youth club in Tyler Street. He was an ex-vicar, and he was a difficult person to talk to, since like all vicars, he marched to a different drummer to the rest of us, but he was pleasant enough. His name was Mr. Saville, and he visited me at home one night. He invited me to try a session at Stratford doing Art, and he could provide some equipment.

So along I went. It was a much bigger building than the Elcaster hut, but the kids were similar. About six volunteered to try some art, but they seemed apathetic, just wanting to sit and chat most of the time. This didn't bother me, as they were not rude at all, just a bit boring. After six weeks they had produced almost nothing of any worth, and I was inclined to give it up. Then Mr. Saville asked me to paint some images on the walls of the main hall. This appealed to me, so I agreed. I used Dylon dyes, as they were the cheapest form of colour and were almost indestructible, so I painted figures like flames on all the inside plastered walls. The kids were supposed to help me, but they lacked skill or enthusiasm, so I ignored them. I was pleased with the end result. I don't think anyone else noticed. I left afterwards, never to return. I ignored Mr. Saville's pleas to go back, I had better things to do.

STEP FIVE -- GROWING PAINS

FUTURE ECCENTRICS

We have interviewed many young people who will become the Characters of Elcaster in future years. So many of the old ones have been dying recently that we feel that we must cultivate the Youth of the Town, and elucidate their embryonic characteristics before they have fully developed; thus we hope to encourage them to blossom and grow into fully-fledged Town Eccentrics in the fullness of time. We do not want them to think of themselves as Characters; anyone who considers themselves one cannot possibly be one, they are just a bore. True eccentrics think that they are normal, and the rest of the world is off its trolley. Here is the first in a long series of interviews with young people.

Interviewer: So, Darren, tell us about yourself

Darren: (Surly silence).

Int. Well, have you any interests?

Dar. Nah.

Int. Have you any hobbies?

Dar. Nah. There's nothin' to do in Elcaster.

Int. How do you view the world situation?

Dar. Dunno.

Int. What do you want out of Life, Darren?

Dar. A Playstation, a Computer, a motor scooter, loads a money, a DVD player, a......

Int. Thank you, Darren. What of your family?

Dar. They're ****ing crap, they are.

Int. How do you find your school?

Dar. I just walks up the road and there it is.
Int. No, I mean what is it like for you?
Dar. Crap. 'S all crap. 'S borin'.
Int. Do you watch TV at all?
Dar. 'S borin', 'S all borin'. Life's borin'.
Int. Thank you, Darren, you've been great!

My own "career" was taking some different turns around this time. The redundancy culture at Lusac Aerospace had become out of hand, and many of us were seriously looking for other jobs. It was difficult for me, because my expertise was in specialist rubbers for high-tech applications, and there were very few places doing such work at this time, at least not in Birmingham. I could go to a rubber factory, but not in my locality, I would have to travel fifty miles, or move house. I could always go back to teaching, of course, but this would mean a large cut in money, and things were a bit costly just then, with our mortgage, teenage children's needs, and so on. Then a miracle happened. A branch of Lusac, Girling Brakes, came round to talk to our lab managers about recruiting the rubber section to work on a project for making brake seals in an innovative way. The Chief Engineer had worked out exactly what he wanted, because he was fed up with buying expensive seals from Lusac Rubber Works in London, who had no interest in doing anything new.

We were asked if we wanted to go, and all three of us said yes. There had been four of us, but my friend Dave had been made redundant some year or so earlier. It would mean that Lusac Aerospace would get rid of three more expensive technical people, and the project looked really interesting. We thought it was a done deal, but the Chief Engineer of Lusac Aerospace came to see me one day.

"Bill, we can't let you go." He hardly knew me. What was this "Bill" stuff? "We have to maintain a polymer presence here at Aerospace, and we think you could do the job. You will be promoted onto a management grade, not just one rung, but two. What do you say?" His face told me that he knew what my answer would be, the smug sod. How, he thought, could I turn down a management grade job? He didn't know me. I didn't even need to think about it for long. "No, I don't think I will, thanks all the same. Just look at the company I'd have to keep!"

His face showed that he had no clue about the meaning of what I had just said. His world was bounded by status, money and his own friends. And engineering. He looked puzzled, and said, "Well, think about it overnight, maybe you'll change your mind when you talk about it with your wife." No chance, i thought, but I smiled politely at him as he strode manfully away, like a Chief Engineer ought.

Next morning, he was puffed up with rage and indignation. Plainly, he now understood the meaning of what I had said about the company I would have to keep. More likely though, he had asked his wife what I had meant, and she had told him. Whatever had brought him to comprehension of my statement, he now said, "We don't want your sort here, Bill. You can go with the others, and good riddance as far as I'm concerned." I told him that the sentiment was entirely mutual. I doubt if he understood that either. He was not a great one with words, that Chief Engineer. He was not even a very good Chief Engineer, and as Lusac was sold to the Americans a few years later, I doubt if he kept his job.

So I bade farewell to Lusac Aerospace and started with Girling, in an old Smith's crisp factory at Tyseley, down the road from where I had been before. It was wonderful. We made a list of all the equipment we would need, and they bought it without question. We set it all up, and started work, to make new materials to make brake seals from. It was the first time in my life that I was doing scientific development work that was properly supported with money, and a management that was listening. Perhaps I had been naive before, I had assumed that was what a technologist did, but Lusac Aerospace was so full of Chiefs all trying to get in on the act that nothing went forward at all. Girling was clearly a different company, with a different ethic. The engineers were in charge, and the accountants worked for them, not the other way round, which is fatal for a scientifically based company. Maybe it was a partnership of accountants and engineers that made it successful, but we were all happy there.

Until Mrs. Thatcher arrived on the scene. Not literally, but she made her presence felt in the engineering world of the Midlands in the early 80s. I did not know it, but our research was partly funded on a government grant, which she cut without warning. So Girling cut the project, one Friday. I was stunned. It had been going so well, the seals were lasting much longer on the test rigs, the moulding method was working, we were about to set up a pilot plant. Suddenly it was at an end. Girling asked us to stay, there was still work, but I felt betrayed. Not by Girling, but by companies and politicians who spoke about science and progress, then kicked you in the knackers when you tried to do it.

I spent the whole weekend lying on my bed and thinking. I had been told by the Chief Engineer at Girling that he was as disappointed as we were, but Margaret Thatcher had ordered all the grants to engineering companies in the Midlands shut down, there and then. It was her way of showing who was boss. She more or less destroyed a lot of engineering manufacturing in the Midlands, causing great unemployment in that area. Was I to be another one unemployed?

Yes, I was. Yet I had another string to my bow, as science teachers were still required. I would take my redundancy money and go back to teaching. I had had enough of the stupidity of industry and politicians. At least I could guarantee a teaching job. So I volunteered to be made redundant on the Monday. I got a little extra as a volunteer. This came from the government. How ironic, but I was getting used to the idiotic ironies of the political world by now. I left a week later, money in my pocket, looking forward to a bit of free time.

I had one day off. The head of my wife's school, hearing I was free to go back to teaching, told me that the Roman Catholic secondary school was looking for a part-time science teacher, if I would care to go along, looking smart. So I went for an interview with the school's head, got the job for two terms, to start on the following Monday. I was part pleased, part bewildered. I wanted more time to think about my changes, and I didn't get it. Too bad, I suppose, I should be thankful I had a job, thousands at that time had not.

So here I was, back again working with kids. I knew I had come home, this was where I belonged. No regrets for my stay in industry, it had paid me much better than teaching, but it had removed the romantic scales from my eyes about how scientists were used in industry. The truth is, in my experience of English industry, scientists were not used, at least not in the way they would be most effective. But in the classroom, I could do what I wanted, within reason. My skills as a teacher were appreciated (or not) by my customers, the kids, and indirectly, their parents. But my skills as a polymer technologist were filtered through the fine weave of manager upon manager, and it only took one to block your effectiveness. So goodbye and good riddance to industry.

I had kept up my attendance at the youth club through all this change. At times it seemed almost a refuge from all the decisions I had to make, as the kids were entirely oblivious to however you might feel. Even when I was quite depressed, they didn't seem to notice. This was a good thing, as it made me just try to behave as usual, and as few demands were made on me that I had not met before, I came away feeling cheered up.

I got on really well at the Catholic Secondary School. It did not matter in the least that I was an agnostic, the Catholics on the staff were not particularly fervent believers either, and I didn't have to go into assemblies, or to Mass on Friday morning. I thought that schools were just the same as when I had left, nine years before. The school was like my old Sec. Mod. in Swindon, except the kids were easier, or maybe I was older. I settled very quickly, and had just begun to enjoy myself when I had to leave.

My contract was only for two terms, as the teacher was returning in September, and I had to find another job, full-time if possible. It was a very bad time for jobs, even teaching science, and I only found one to apply for, in Erdington, Birmingham. One of the teachers at my school came up to me, to warn me. He said. "Don't take that job, Bill. Stockland Green is a terrible school. I know because I went there on my teaching practice. The head is a liar, and there is a dreadful atmosphere. Don't go!"

But I thought I had no choice, It was the only job I had seen, so I went for the interview. The head seemed all right, and the head of science was a small Welshman who I thought I could work with. They told me the school was almost a grammar school, with academic aspirations. I said I could do that, I had taught A Levels at St. Stephen's. The only odd thing was they interviewed me at the end of school, with no pupils around. I thought nothing of it. I accepted the job.

My colleagues said nothing at the Catholic school except to congratulate me on getting a job, any job, in that climate of 1980, Thatcher's Dark Age. So I prepared myself for the long drag into Erdington every morning, through Spaghetti Junction, past Birmingham's waste land of abandoned factories. I started at the beginning of September.

I soon found out why they had interviewed my at the end of the day. The pupils looked awful. They were down-at-heel, scruffy, lacklustre and not very bright. What was all that about 'almost a grammar school'? It was the reverse. I spoke to one of the staff about this. He laughed, and said, "The head is a great self-deluder. He looks like a liar, but he truly believes the bullshit he spouts, and we have to try to put it into practice. You'll get used to it. Or leave, like most of them do."

It was much worse than St. Stephen's. The morale of

the staff was about zero, there was no camaraderie, they all left as soon as the afternoon bell went. They knew there were no other jobs out there, so they had to just stick it out. Worse than that, my head of department decided to try to make me a scapegoat for the failures of his science department. I was not used to this, teachers cheating and lying about each other, but the plain fact was there. The little cheat was complaining about me to the Head before I had been there a month. He did as little work as he could get away with, spending some time with a pal of his, a police patrol car copper, who came in for coffee, and they would chat brazenly about "the nig-nogs", and how they would send the lot back home. This man was then going out to teach these 'nig-nogs', despising them. How could he possibly teach them thinking as he did?

The West Indian kids were different to any I had taught before. They were stroppy, hated being told off, and very lazy, especially the boys. But this wasn't their fault, not all of it. Erdington was a very poor area, most households had no adult working, the men tended to abandon their families. No wonder they were not motivated to work, there were no jobs even if they did well in their exams. Most of them did badly, and I found out that no-one had passed GCE Physics the previous year. Some grammar school!

I kept on with my youth club work doggedly. It made me much more tired than before, because I was working with difficult kids all day long. By comparison, the Elcaster kids were easy, much slower than the City kids I taught. But after a few months, the inevitable happened. I got clinically depressed, and my doctor wanted me to take time off.

Depression had happened to me before, in short bursts, and I was well used to taking antidepressants, which didn't do much for me, but dulled the sharp edge a bit. I had so little spare energy that I had to stop going to the youth club, I just couldn't face it. I used to go to bed at 9.30, and wake up still tired at 7.00 a.m., dreading the long haul into Erdington. I thought I was totally useless as a teacher, and it seemed that my head of department would have agreed.

Later reflection made me think about my time at my prep school, Thorpe House. In Stockland Green I was again in the situation of the dog in the inescapable cage, punished repeatedly for reasons it cannot understand, so it goes into a depression and cannot respond to anything. In my case, I thought I could not give up the job because we needed the money, and my pride would not let me either. I was being punished by the lying head, and the head of department, as well as my own conscience, and I could not see how to respond. So my subconscious tactic was to roll over and become depressed, do nothing. Then, like the dog, things happen. For the dog, the experiment is over, and it is treated normally, But it doesn't recover quickly, it takes some time. This is also what happened to me.

I got some help. A very nice man, a PhD in Physics who

had been made redundant, was sent to help me in the classroom. He told me almost at once that there was nothing wrong with my teaching, that I was better than most he had seen, in other schools as well as this one, and I just had to believe more in myself. But I could not. When you are in the grip of serious depression, you are incapable of seeing anything objectively. I just knew I was a failure, and no-one could convince me otherwise. My doctor persuaded me to stop and have some time at home. I told him If I did that, I would never go back. He said "Good!" He didn't have to pay my mortgage, though.

So began the most miserable period of my life so far. I sat at home, getting sick pay for a few months, then only the money the government gave to the long-term sick. I knew I was finished. My employers, Birmingham Education, seemed to have lost all interest in me. I stayed at home, reading when I could, doing a bit of cooking for the family, not talking to anyone except my poor wife. I could not have gone to the youth club to save my life.

WRESTLING WITH THE DRAGON

I have had a dragon in my life for over fifty years now. It is a part of me, it will never leave me, and by now I don't want it to go. It spends a lot of time now asleep, but I know it is there, I can hear it breathing if I keep very still. I am no longer afraid of it. How should I be afraid of something that is part of me?

It first made its presence known when I was twenty two, and had got my degree from college, and was planning on getting married. It came suddenly, it overwhelmed me with its ferocity. I could no longer think, I could not work, I was too miserable. Now I know it has a name, but I didn't know it then. It is called Depression. Nobody can know what it is like unless they have suffered from it a bit themselves, and even then they will only know their own, and not mine. I have found out that nearly everyone suffers from it at some time in their lives, whether it is called Grief, Accidie, or whatever. I believe it is part of being human, but no-one talks about it much. It is at present regarded as a Mental Illness. I think this is too simplistic, and it shuts sufferers out from being part of the human race. This is wrong. It is no more an illness than being a teenager is, or getting old. It makes money for the therapists, drug companies, and so on, but none of them get to the heart of the matter: it is normal, and must be coped with by the sufferer, with help.

My first dragon attack ended when I changed my life, temporarily. Instinct got me away from my dismal London flat, into the countryside on a bicycle, and then a job planting trees. Slowly the dragon receded into his lair. I got married as I had planned, got a new job teaching, but I was afraid it would come back.

It did return, seven years later. By this time, I knew enough to go to a doctor, who told me to 'pull myself together', in a kindly way. This was useless advice. I would have given my right hand to do that, but I could not.

It was not until I came to Elcaster that I got any real help. A local doctor, who might be embarrassed if I named him, but he knows who he is, took me seriously. He gave me antidepressants. The relief I felt, that it was not my fault, that something could be done, was marvellous, but not enough to drive away the dragon. The pills did help a bit. like taking aspirin for a piercing headache, but they did not get to the root. Time did that, always. It lasted however long it wanted, then slowly receded.

I was no longer afraid of another attack. They came along, with no pattern to them, and I coped. I went to work, I related to people, and it took me a long time to realise that most people had no idea of how I felt inside. It doesn't show, the presence of the dragon. The battle is entirely in my head.

Maybe not entirely. It matters what I do as well. I found it important to keep trying to lead a normal life, do things, even though I could not think straight. I could think straight enough to manage, just. My doctor once said, 'let the drugs do the work'. I knew this was not quite right. There were things I had to do, but I did not know what they were. I had to keep trying.

Now I am retired, the dragon's attacks do not matter so much. But they still come. I have looked and looked for a cause, but found none that is certain. I find it helps to try to help others, which is why I am writing this. I have found Stoicism, which tells me that I should pursue Virtue, and be indifferent to those things I can do nothing about. It is hard to be indifferent to my dragon, he demands attention to his feelings of dread and fear, but I try. I know the feelings are only an illusion in my head.

Without my dragon, I would have been a different person. But I am human and all humans have our own dragon. We must learn to love them, they are us.

I woke up a little in the early Summer, when a friend made me go and help him on his farm, getting the hay crop in. He had no people working for him, and he could not pay me much, but he thought the hard work and the fresh air might do me good. It certainly did, although at first it almost killed me. Then I had a letter from the Erdington school to tell me I had been made redundant from the school. Thanks a bunch, Stockland Green, you know how to kick a man when he's down. But in the letter came a form, which told me I was eligible for a grant for retraining. An idea dawned on me (the first for months). I would go and do my PGCE (Post Graduate Certificate of Education), a teaching course at a local university, even though I already was a qualified teacher. Luckily, Birmingham turned me down, but Warwick accepted me. They thought it odd that I wanted a qualification that I already had, but I explained that I didn't want another degree, one was enough for anyone. I wanted time to teach, talk about teaching, and be watched teaching, so I could be a better teacher. They bought that idea, and so I started there one October morning, a student at a proper

University, not a Polytechnic, for the first time in my life.

I was happy again, on the very first day. The depression fell away like an old skin, and I felt born again. I was in the right place at the right time for the right reasons. I knew that I could teach, but I wanted to learn to do it better. I began to rethink my reasons for teaching. I eventually came to three points that I had to do that would make me a better teacher.

One, I had to love my subject, be really interested in it, all aspects of it, not just the syllabus. This was easy for me, as I had always been a kind of scientist, questioning everything, seeing what evidence is around for saying what is being said. You have to make them think.

Two. You have to communicate that interest in words that your audience, the clients, the pupils, can understand. Explain if they are puzzled. Repeat a different way, use stories, images, parables, even for quite mundane things.

Three. You have to like your customers. Every one of them. No exceptions. This is quite hard with some stroppy rude youngsters, but you can always find something to like about them, even if it's their persistence. Never use sarcasm, it hurts for too long. You don't have to love them, that is reserved for family and friends. You cannot be their friend, you have to be their teacher. That is why you are there.

Being now full of energy, I went back to the youth club

one Tuesday night. The hut was dark, so I went to the bar in the Grogg Hall. They were all there, looking very glum. I sat down And they told me they had packed up the youth club that very night. They had had enough. I asked Jim what had happened. He told me.

" The trustees have made it harder and harder for us over the last year. Endless complaints about the noise, about the behaviour of the kids outside the hut, damage and interruptions to other groups, and they put our rent up several times. They made it quite plain that we are not welcome. They have told us that the Cadets want our hut, so there is no room for us. It's not true, but that's what they say, so what can we do? The County Youth Service do not help, they will not send anyone to work with us, they just keep repeating that the Grogg is there as a youth club, and they won't help us. They won't even put in a word to the trustees, they say that's our job. And the kids have become more difficult and ruder. They say it's boring, but we have no money to take them on trips, so what can we do? We have just become fed up. Time to pack it in, we all think."

The others agreed with Jim. They told me sad tales of awful things the kids had said and done. I offered to come back and help, but they just shook their heads. They had gone too far down, and could not come back. We had a last drink together and went on our respective ways.

I was furious. Just when I wanted to try out some ideas

on kids I was getting from Warwick University, there was nobody to practice on. And how could the Grogg do that, set up as it was in its constitution that it was to be a youth club. They were not doing their job. They were being snobbish as only middle-class authorities can be. But I could do nothing on my own except fume.

Later in that year, I almost burst into flames with anger. I read in the local paper that the trustees had appointed a manager at a salary of £10,000 a year. Ten thousand! And they refused to pay a youth worker which would cost a tenth of that! I wrote a letter of complaint to the paper, putting my point of view, saying it was disgraceful behaviour on the part of the trustees, and what were they going to do about the fact that there was now no youth club at all in the Town. Thanks to the deliberate discouragement by the Grogg trustees of the existing youth workers, who had done a brilliant job despite all the discouragements running a youth club brings.

I did not expect any result, but I got one I hadn't expected. A large man with a fierce expression came walking up to my back door a few days after the letter was published. His name was Jeff Young, a digger driver at the time, also known as Swanny. He didn't beat about the bush, he wasn't that sort. He hardly even introduced himself. He came straight to the point.

"I read your letter, and it made me mad. You're quite

right, there should be a youth club here in the Town, and it should be at the Grogg Hall. We've got to do something about it. You and me. All right?"

I realise now that it was at that precise point that my fire was lit. A lot of things came suddenly together. My experience with schools both good and bad, my wanting to work with ordinary people (and Jeff was ordinary in one way, but later I was to learn how extraordinary he really was), my desire to do something in the Town for the 'ordinary' people, my liking for kids, my desire to teach not just science, the knowledge of how little was done for the kind of kids that came to the youth club, but above all the sense of injustice that the behaviour of the Grogg trustees ignited in me. "From those that have nothing, even that which they have shall be taken away," is what the Bible says. It was monstrously unfair to close the youth club, it was class prejudice of the worst kind.

All these thoughts and feeling went through my mind as I listened to Jeff. I knew I could work with him, he came from the Conway Estate and everyone there knew him and he knew everyone. I agreed with him, we had to do something. And we did.

It was far from clear what we could do at first. Jeff would blow off steam about the Grogg Hall, but I knew it was useless to talk to them. They had made up their minds not to have a youth club, and there it would stay. They thought that the Grogg Hall was a business, and had to run at a profit. Youth clubs only paid rent, and not much of that. The youths caused damage, annoyed the other customers, and generally made the place untidy. They gave it a Bad Name, so it was best if they just never came onto the site. The trustees at that time were two local men, one a shopkeeper who owned and ran the local newsagents on the High Street. The other was an elderly gentleman whose father had been the editor of the local newspaper in the days when such a position meant something. He did not work, but owned a lot of run-down property in the Town. The first, Derek Collet, was cunning and ambitious, and he wound the other, Aubrey Gwinnet, round his little finger. Aubrey was gullible and trusting, never married, he just wanted to be the mildly eccentric Gentleman-about-Town. It was Collett who wanted rid of the youth club. He had come from the Conway himself, but saw himself as having risen above that, and was now at least one class higher. He did not want any reminder of his humble origins, since all the parents of our kids knew him when he was just one of them. He hated that. There was a Grogg family member who also came occasionally, a nephew of the original David Grogg, called Dennis. Nobody ever met him, he was plainly not interested in Elcaster and its affairs, and it seemed that his role was to protect the Grogg family name. He was a stockbroker from Surrey, and must have believed that all Elcastrians were country hicks, ignorant of How Things Were Done in his elite world.

So Collett's action in kicking out the youth club would

have been agreed by the others. There were also some other dignitaries who sat and advised the two trustees, but they had no executive powers, so it would not matter if they had disagreed or not. The curious fact was that the constitution of the Grogg Hall clearly stated that it was to be run 'for the benefit of the youth of the Town'. There was even a board with that written on it at the Grogg Hall entrance. This wording used to make Jeff huff and puff with rage, but I knew we had to be more cunning to get what we wanted. Which was a youth club back at the Grogg Hall. It might take time, but we would get it.

There were other buildings in the Town that would have been suitable. One was owned by the Town Council, and it had become vacant. Another group was also keen on having it, so Jeff and I went along to a Town Council meeting one night, to put our case. Jeff made me speak, as he said I sounded posh, and he would only get angry. So I did. I used the phrase, "we will help keep the kids off the streets", when one of the councillors stood up, a Londoner who had founded the Trades and Labour Club, and I knew he had the community at heart.

"Just a minute, Mr. Bayley. What's wrong with the Street? Why should we keep them off it? I did all my courting in the East End on the Street. There's nuffin' wrong with the Street."

I had to concede that he was right, but everyone there knew what I meant. The Town Council said they would think about it.

We were disappointed when they let it to the other group. I think there had been some rumbles of dissent from those that lived nearby, so the council played safe and denied it to us. But we did get some press coverage from it, and some people were saying it was a shame that the Grogg couldn't see its way to letting a youth club in. Collett replied that there was no-one to run it now, as the County would not send anyone, and the previous workers had left. Anyway, the local volunteers were not qualified to run a youth club. He thought he was on safe ground, but Jeff and I pricked up our ears.

Another building owned by the Town Council became vacant, and I was invited to go with the mayor, a local farmer, to see if it was suitable. So I went, and was surprised to find Mr. Collett there with the mayor. We all agreed that the building was not suitable, being damp and run-down. Then the mayor and Collett said, "If only there were someone to run a club, they might be allowed back to the Grogg. Someone suitably qualified, of course."

It was my moment. My guardian angel had led me to this point, on this day, with those two listening. I had to speak. I felt the words stick in my throat, but I spat them out a last. "I'll do it. I will run a youth club at the Grogg Hall. Give me some time to get people together. I'm a qualified teacher, which is qualification enough to run a club"

They looked surprised. I don't think either of them knew I had been a teacher, and they probably regretted what they had just said. Collett was trying to look generous in the mayor's eyes, and the mayor had nothing to lose either way, except he didn't now have to find a building for a youth club. I asked Collett when I could meet with the trustees. He waffled a bit, but the mayor was looking at him, so he told me to come to the next trustees meeting.

Jeff was really pleased. That night he went to the Trades and Labour Club and recruited five volunteers. I don't know how he did it, but he could be a hard man to refuse. We all met in the White Lion the next week. There were two married couples, both with kids of youth club age, and a friend of Jeff's who was younger. Jeff introduced us, and I could tell they were suspicious of my accent, and of my being a teacher. None of them got on well with teachers. I had to reassure them. I told them that I would not regard it as MY youth club, all decisions would be made by a committee meeting every month, and I was sure we could make it a success. It was Jeff that swung it, of course. If he trusted me, then they could give it a try. So we had seven volunteers to try to make it work.

Then we realised we had no kids. How would we put it around that a new club was opening? I had an idea. I had just got a portable video camera of my own, to use in schools if possible, but it was great fun making silly videos with the family. So I suggested we got as many kids in one place one day at half-term, asked them on camera what they wanted from a youth club, so we had some ideas to start with. We would also ask the Press to be there, and a week or so later we would show the video to the Town Council, and get the Press there again.

It worked like a dream. There were lots of kids, of all ages, and they were eager to appear on TV, as they put it. They made all kinds of promises, even though I warned them that what they said was recorded and could be used later as evidence when we had a youth club. The Press were good too, and wrote a very sparky piece for the local paper, the Elcaster Chronic. (Really the Chronicle, but everyone left off the last two letters). We hired the local Baptist Hall, and asked the Town Council, and quite a lot came. We had some tame kids hand round biscuits and tea, and the councillors were all smiles, but guarded about promises. We got another good press article out of that, so all we had to do now was fix the date to open at the Grogg.

I thought it would be easy. Trustees and mayors don't make promises often, but when they do they usually keep them. They have reputations to preserve, after all. So when I was summoned to the trustees committee meeting, I went with a light heart. We were getting a good press, people knew about what we were trying to do and were very supportive. They always support a youth club, just so long as it isn't coming near them.

I sat down at the foot of a long table. There were about ten people around it, including Mr. Collett at the head. He welcomed me, and introduced me to the others, some of whom I already knew.

"I would like to put a proposition to you, Mr. Bayley. What would you say if we put on a Youth Cafe, rather than a youth club? It would be better all round, don't you think. It would be easier to run, our own staff could lend a hand. What do you say to that idea?"

"I think it is a first-class idea. Thank you very much for your offer, and we would be glad to support you. But we want a youth club. That's what we have promised the kids and their parents, and that's what you promised yourself, Mr. Collett."

His face changed, darkened to a more threatening hue. "I think you'll find our offer is a very generous one. A Cafe would be most acceptable to our committee, and I am sure to your prospective members. Perhaps you don't appreciate the difficulties of having a youth club on this site, Mr. Bayley."

"Oh, please call me Bill. Everyone else does. I'm sure there are considerable difficulties, but we will sort out most of them for you in the club itself, on the night. Anyone who is troubled by any of our members must come to us immediately to make their complaint, and we can do something about it. It will be no good if they leave it until next week, we cannot act then. It must be sorted then and there. There is bound to be some trouble, that's the nature of teenagers. After all, it does say in your constitution that you should provide for the

Youth of Elcaster, doesn't it? What other difficulties do you anticipate, Mr. Collett?"

I had stymied him. He couldn't think of any. He didn't know that I had seen their constitution, either. In fact, I hadn't seen it, I was guessing. I started again. "I have come here to arrange a starting date, and the rent we shall pay, and how it is to be paid. Now, let's get down to it, shall we?"

One of the trustee advisors, a pompous little man who resembled Uriah Heep, addressed me in such a way as he thought would put me in my place. "Tell us, Mr. Bayley, since you seem to know so much about how to run a youth club, exactly how would you do it?"

"Certainly Mr. Onions. Would you like my five minute summary, or my twenty-minute talk?"

There was a pregnant silence. I took off my wristwatch, and put it on the table in front of me. "I take it by your silence that you want my twenty-minute talk. Here is what I would do." I talked for precisely twenty minutes about teenagers, how to handle them, what kinds of activities we would do, how we would have monthly meetings, and so on. It was easy for me, I had been a teacher, I could waffle til the cows came home. They listened to me without saying a word. I saw that they were getting restless, but I ploughed on. I was not going to be put in my place by a little man called Onions.

I picked up my watch when I had finished. "Is that enough? I could go on, if you want. Have you any questions for me?" They hadn't. How surprising. We fixed a date for the opening in about four weeks time. We were to have the large hut that was also used as a rehearsal room, but it would do for our purposes. "Thank you, gentlemen. I shall give that date to the Press. We shall try to keep our word, to pay for any permanent damage done, to sweep it every time we use it, and not to interfere with anything left by other groups. I think that's all as far as I am concerned. I bid you good night. And let me know when your Youth Cafe is opening. We might like to help you with it." I left before they could say anything more.

Jeff and the others were really pleased. "I thought they might trick you out of their promise, Bill, but you got what we wanted. That Cafe will never happen, but our youth club will." We made preparations, bought some games, a small pool table, a dart board, and a few other gadgets for them to play on. I went to the manager, who was most helpful, to my surprise. He clearly thought there ought to be a youth club at the Grogg, as he was an Elcaster man himself. He was easy to deal with, we made arrangements to store some of our stuff during the week, and we agreed to pay the rent monthly in advance. We shook hands cordially when I left.

There was still one last hurdle to jump; the opening night. We planned a quiet start, just the helpers there, with the kids, getting to know each other. Nothing spectacular, no

drums, no shouting, no singing. So one Autumn Thursday evening I turned up at the hut, to find about twenty would-be members waiting outside. They were noisy, and excited. Not as excited as I was. What if it didn't work? What if they were so badly behaved we couldn't control them? Worse, what if nobody came? Well, that problem was not to be, there they were. We had said they could go in at seven, and it was ten minutes to go. Then along came the manager. I greeted him, but his face was unsmiling. I asked him, "What's up, David? Something happened?"
He looked at me. "The key is lost."

I gasped ironically. The hut had been open during the day, I knew. I looked him in the eye. His gaze slid away, and I knew he was lying. He was not a dishonest man, so I knew who had given him the orders not to let us in. Testing our resolve, was he?

"Oh, I'm so sorry the key is lost, David. I'll tell you what. If that door isn't open by seven as promised, I am ringing the reporter from the Chronic to bring a photographer to take a picture of all these kids waiting for you to keep your promise, made publicly. I shall be pleased to give an interview too. You've got five minutes."

The key was 'found', and we went in for our first night as the Alcester Youth Club. David the manager never mentioned the 'lost' key again. We both knew what a cheap trick he was forced to play, but it didn't work. How could it?

We were on our way.

STEP SIX -- OBSTRUCTIONS

THE CHRISTMAS WASP

The little wasp awoke from his winter sleep behind the top rafters of the old stable. He stretched his legs one by one. He could tell by the light it was not yet Spring. So why had he woken? He waved his antennae over the edge of the rafter and sniffed the air. Something strange there. Some scent, exotic. He looked over.

He saw three men walking slowly up to a small crib, in which a baby lay sleeping. These men were clothed in rich garments, and they all had crowns on their heads. They looked like Kings, yet they were walking with their heads bent, as if the baby was an even greater King than them. There were other figures in the gloom around the crib, the wasp saw, one was clearly the mother. There were animals as well, all looking towards the baby as if he were some kind of God. The wasp thought he saw huge figures in white with wings, and he heard a kind of music in the air, coming from nowhere, yet everywhere. The wasp felt awed, as if he were in the presence of something beyond him, something so great he could not comprehend it. Yet he felt great joy, greater than he had ever felt. He thought his tiny heart would burst with happiness.

Suddenly he knew what he must do. The Kings were clearly bringing gifts to the baby, so he must do the same. Yet what had he to give? He looked around him, and saw a crumb of bread he had put on the rafter in the Autumn, ready to eat when he woke in the Spring. I will give him that, thought the wasp. It is all I have, but it will comfort the babe, and I will fly above him in intricate patterns, to amuse and delight him. I will make him laugh and show him that wasps have gifts and talents to bring to the World, as well as human Kings.

The tiny wasp struggled to pick up the crumb in his jaws, and finally managed to secure it. He launched himself from the rafter, and noted how his buzzing blended with the celestial music in a quite delightful way.

He fought to keep hold of the crumb of bread as he sailed through the air towards the crib. His strength was low, as he had slept for three months, yet by a supreme effort he kept control, swinging first left, then correcting himself by swinging right. His wings kept a frantic beating against the night air in the stable, and the strange scent was making him dizzy, and his eyes were running as well. He found more strength from somewhere, from outside himself in some magical way, and his small heart leapt in joy as he approached the baby.

The baby had seen him, and was smiling and stretching out his tiny arms towards him. I am coming, my Lord, I am coming, sang the wasp, as he started to perform some clever aerobatics for the baby's amusement. Up to the left and roll, down to the right and spin, the wasp was really getting into his best ever performance.

The animals had noticed him too, and raised their heads to watch his progress. They were not too sure of wasps, especially those that came out in the winter, but they saw how he soared and dipped, and were comforted that he meant no harm to them.

The Kings had stopped around the crib, which was lit by a strange light that came from nowhere, like the heavenly music, which was swelling in volume. It's for me, thought the wasp, the climax will be when I land at the baby's feet and pay him homage with my minuscule gift. His joy was without bounds.

Joseph stepped forward and swatted the wasp to the ground, and stamped on it. "Damned wasps, always getting where they're not wanted!", he said with an apologetic smile to the Kings. They nodded in agreement.

We started well. We had a nucleus of volunteers, seven of us, and we ran the youth club once a week for two hours, seven thirty to nine-thirty. We tried to get the members to help clear up afterwards, but they always seemed to slide out with excuses, so the adults did it. It was a chance to talk about the happenings of that night, who was rude, who was funny, who were in love, who were absent. It was tiring, but in a pleasant way, and we felt we were getting something done that was worth while. The two couples had their own kids as members of the club, so we got feedback from what they said, and what the kids told us on the night.

We had a committee meeting every month, at the Trades & Labour saloon bar. I was the chairman and took notes as minutes. We all agreed that any adult who helped at the club was automatically on the committee, but it didn't matter if they came or not. All of them did. I made a personal rule, that nothing was ever decided without putting it to the committee and voting on it. I had another rule too, that I told everyone. Nobody could suggest doing something if they weren't prepared to front it themselves, or had found somebody to do that. I was fed up at other committees with people saying, "I think we should do...." and then wrangling about who would do it, or worse, nothing being done at all. So if you wanted to suggest something, then you had to do it, or don't even bring it up. Another rule I practised as chairman was that we didn't talk about stuff that was not on the agenda. If we wanted to chat and gossip, which is a highly important activity of committees, this was done after the meeting closed, and we sat around with our drinks and changed the world. They regarded me as a very strict chairman, but I got things done, they had to admit.

The matter of Rules came up early on. One rule we made was that any adult present could expel a member for any reason they thought fit. normally rudeness or violent overactivity, but that the matter had to be brought up at the next committee meeting. No member was ever to be excluded permanently. This was because they would then become an uncontrollable nuisance. We tried having youth members on the committee, but they came a few times, got bored, and never came again. We soon gave up on that idea. But the kids and the adults wanted rules for behaviour within the club, and I said there were only three rules needed. One, you must respect each other as well as yourself. Two, you must treat the building and the stuff in it with respect, and not abuse it. Third, use your common sense, and obey the Law of the Land. These were the only rules necessary, I said. This was based on Jesus' teaching about the Two Commandments. Love God, and love thy neighbour as thyself. In this case, God was replaced by the environment, but it seemed adequate to me.

The committee members disagreed with me, and I was outvoted. We had an evening in the club where the members were invited to make the rules they wanted themselves. We split them into Girls and Boys, and gave them big sheets of paper and marker pens. After a lot of vigourous discussion, especially from the boys, they drew up two sets of rules. The boys' rules were terse and to the point, the girls' were couched in flowery language, but were more or less the same as the boys', except they disliked swearing, and the boys didn't care, but they agreed to put it on the Rule List. These rules were pinned to the wall, and admired by all, except me. Half an hour later, a boy came up to me. "Bill, Rob's swearing at me. Can you stop him?" My answer surprised him. "It's your rule, you enforce it. I'm not a policeman, or your parent. It doesn't affect me. You do something about it." He went away puzzled, to find an adult who would do what he wanted.

I brought up my Three Rules again at the next meeting. There was more discussion, and they agreed that enforcing the rules was the hard bit. After another meeting they agreed to take down the rules, and try my method 'just for a month'. I never heard another word about rules. A few years later, with a few new members, the new ones suggested we had some rules, so we went through the motions again, with the same results. I heard one adult explaining the principle to a new member as if it had been her idea. I hoped that by this time, that was what it was.

One of the women asked me if she could do the training provided by the County, and so get paid for the session. I said this might be a good idea, and so she went on the three-hour course once a month. I asked her how it was going after her first session, and she was cagey. After her third session she told me she might give up. I asked her why. "Well, they don't seem to know much about how youth clubs actually work, do they?" I asked her what she meant. "There are all these old blokes telling us they have loads of experience in youth clubs, right, but it turns out they haven't been in one for years, certainly not running one. They tell you a load of bollocks, excuse my French. They said we were to write out a youth club programme for a night, so I wrote out what we had done here last week. Then they say, Oh no, that's far too much, that's enough for a month.' When I tell them it's what we actually did last week, they just laugh at me, Bill. I ent going again. Sod the money, it's a waste of my time."

She was right, of course. It's so easy to pontificate about the theory of youth clubs when you are not in one, and you have to face the difficulties of youth in the raw. That's what they were doing there, they were men who couldn't do the job, or were too old, and the County had to employ them somehow, so it was they that did the training. It's the same in teaching, and probably a lot more activities like painting, acting and so no. Unless you are engaged in doing it very recently, you forget the difficulties that make it almost impossible. All you remember is the good bits that worked, mainly by chance, and not that often. I told her, you're getting the best possible training here at our club. On the job, in front of other adults and members, with discussion about what goes wrong (and it always does) afterwards. I had great respect for the County workers who were actually doing youth work, and very little for those that were advisors, or managers.

We never did have any help from the County, until toward the end of our life as a youth club. Sometimes a worker came to visit us, and they were always pleasant but noncommittal about sending any paid workers. That was wise, of them, because were were going well, and we would not have fitted the County's concept of How to Run A Youth Club. We were doing it, and they left well alone. They used to ask what help we got from the Greig Trust, and the answer was always, none. We paid the rent, sorted out the problems on the night, and we got few complaints.

So at this point we come to the central theme of this book, How to Run a Youth Club in Ten Easy Steps. And here is how. Just do it. Follow your nose, your instincts. First, you must want to do it, and that's all you need. You will fall flat at first, but pick yourself up and do it again, like riding a bicycle. Don't bother reading books about it, not until afterwards. Just do it. And don't think you have been conned into buying this book by it's title. You never believed it could be learned in Ten Easy Steps, did you? If you did, perhaps to might be amused. It could be said that you deserve to lose your money. A fool and his money are soon parted.

The adults thought it a good idea if I went on the Board of Trustees at the Grogg, just to protect the club against what had happened before. So we packed the Annual General Meeting, and I was elected as a trustee, ousting a rather surprised shopkeeper who had been asked to join as nobody else wanted the post. I did not look forward to the first trustee meeting, having crossed swords with them already. I was armed and on the defensive right from the start.

The trustees had changed a bit since I had known them at the last youth club. There had been some fuss in the papers about queries on the accounts, and the Charity Commission had insisted that there should be more than three trustees, so each group using the Grogg should have a representative on the committee. This meant that there were about a dozen people around a table, chaired still by Mr. Collett, and of course there was now a manager as well.

It was clear to me from the outset that all the committee were interested in was making money. Or rather, not losing too much of it. So every activity was scrutinised to see if it "paid its way", and the youth club was one that was under the microscope at once. We had no difficulty paying the rent that the Grogg required, but who would pay for the damages inflicted by the terrifying feral youths? The answer was that there was no damage. We had told the manager to tell every group that met on the same night as we did to report any trouble at once to us, the youth club organisers. We stood a chance of catching the culprits, but if they left it to the next day, or next week, there was no chance, and we could do little. This worked well. The Operatics often complained that kids were at the windows making faces as they rehearsed their solo arias, and we used to chase them away easily enough. We did not complain about the garbled warbling sounds that inflicted damage to our sensitive ears, we let that slide. We were generous to a fault, you can see.

Nobody on the trustees committee had anything to say about the youth club. They never asked how it was going, never asked if we wanted any help, never offered the slightest encouragement, which was rather neglectful of them, since they had been set up as a youth club, after all. I knew the actual score, though. As long as they took no interest in us, we were safe. There was no chance they could make life difficult for us and throw us off the site like they had done to the last club.

They were a very dull bunch, though. There were no ideas about how to act as a community centre, no concept of who their clients were and what they wanted, no sense that the Grogg Hall was a charity serving a community. The prevailing idea seemed to be that the Grogg was doing everyone a favour in just existing, and people should be grateful to get anything at all. The provision of squash courts and a sports hall done a few years before were commercial ventures, and should have paid for themselves by now. Of course, neither of them did, but this was seen as the base ingratitude of the populace, unable to grasp the opportunities offered them by a bounteous Grogg Trust. I thought all this was pure rubbish, but what was the point of saying so? I was in a minority of one, a 'do-gooder' amongst hard-headed businessmen, what chance did I have of being listened to? Of course, they were not so much hard-headed as thick-headed. If they ran their tiny businesses like they ran the Grogg, they would have been bust in a month. But of course it was not their money they were risking, it was the Grogg's, and at that time there was plenty of it left. They could afford to gamble, and if they lost, so what? The Grogg would pay. They never offered any of this money to the groups, just spent it on ventures for which they could take the credit. The trouble was there was nothing successful, so there was no credit to take.

There was a member of the Grogg family on the trustees board, one Dennis Grogg, the nephew of the original David Grogg who had set up the Hall in memory of his dead wife. He looked like the Young Mister Grace out of 'Are You Being Served', but without any of his pleasantness. He was humourless and snappy, a dapper dresser, fastidious and fussy. He plainly despised everyone around the table as country bumpkins, not capable of running a whelk stall. He made it obvious that he had no interest in Elcaster at all, and was merely there to protect the name of Grogg. I suspected there might be another reason, but I could not think what it could be, as I was innocent of the cunning ways of charities. He was a stockbroker from Surrey, very wealthy, never offering any money to the Trust, nor any encouragement. He never enquired about the youth club, nor socialised with the other trustees. I summed him up as being rather a nasty little squirt, to be avoided at all costs. He was certainly not a man to go to if the youth club were to be in trouble, rather the reverse. Derek Collett was odiously sycophantic towards him, "Yes, Mr. Grogg", "No, Mr. Grogg", "You are so right there, Mr. Grogg". It made me quite sick to hear him, and most of the other trustees were almost as bad. It occurred to me that this was the origin of the attitude that Elcaster should be grateful for the Grogg. This odious little toad had infected the whole committee with his loathsome rich-man's morality. I left the trustees board after only a year, and I felt my time had been wasted there. I had made good friends with David Rick, the manager, and knew he would warn me if the youth club was to be attacked again.

I made good relations with all the Grogg staff, including the caretaker, a character straight out of Harold Pinter, but with a local slant. He had a house provided on the site, and was very touchy about the hours he worked. It was more than your life was worth to try to contact him outside working hours. He would snap at you and scuttle back into his hobbit-hole. He did work hard, and was often seen carrying chairs and arranging the stacking of tables late into the night after an evening event. Treated right, he would do anything for you, provided it was in working time, or in paid overtime.

David Rick, the new manager, became a friend. I used to sit in his office and listen to his woes, and they were always about one thing -- Collett, the Chair of trustees. Technically his employers were the whole board of trustees, but they were a lazy lot and they left it to Collett to manage the staff. Collett was a most devious and unpredictable character, and he would change his mind as often as he changed his socks. It drove poor David Rick crazy, since he never knew where he was with him. One minute he was all friendly, calling him 'David', and the next he was delivering a reprimand for something he had not done, or had failed to do, but had been told the opposite. I tried to give David Rick the tools to get to grips with such a man, since I had met a few in my time in work. It was in vain; David Rick was honest and straightforward, and Collett was the opposite, as well as being the Boss, a role he relished and abused daily.

One particular conversation sticks in my memory. David was finding the takings on the bar were always down, and expensive drinks, like spirits, went missing too. He had investigated, checked the staff completely, put in a system so that the staff could not possibly be responsible, but still money and liquor were short.

"Well, David, let's do a Sherlock Holmes on this. Who has a key to the bar?"

"There are two, Bill. One's mine, and the other Mr. Collett has."

"And there's no chance of there being another?"

"No, we changed the locks only two months ago."

"And nobody has broken in? No signs of forced entry?"

"Not at all. It's a complete mystery. Mind you, Mr. Collett doesn't seem to mind all that much."

"Very well. Sherlock Holmes says, when you have eliminated the probable, what remains, however impossible, must be the Truth."

"What does that mean, Bill?"

"It means that Collett is taking the stuff. He probably thinks it's his anyway."

"Oh no, Bill, that cannot be right. Mr. Collett would never do anything like that."

"Why not, David? What's to stop him?"

"Well, he's the manager. He's an honest man. He's a ..."

"A gentleman, were you going to say? I've met 'gentlemen' who would steal your grandma and look innocent. No, David, it's him. It's obvious. Ask him, if you don't believe me."

"Oh, I could never do that, Bill. It wouldn't be right."

And he never did ask him, because to his way of thinking it wasn't right. It is a very Midlands attitude, the Boss must be honest and trustworthy, otherwise, how did he get to be the Boss? If you question the integrity of the Bosses, then the whole world is threatened, and anarchy is just around the corner. The money and drink never did stop going missing from the bar. David stopped worrying about it, since Collett didn't press him. It was this fact alone that pointed to the culprit, as sure as day follows night. Elementary, my dear Rick. Collett's honesty came under more severe scrutiny later, with a different outcome.

The youth club was going like a train. We had raised a bit of money by jumble sales, enough to pay the rent, and Jeff confessed to us all that his lifelong ambition was to run a youth club, just him in charge. We had our reservations, but you did not voice them to Jeff, he was too big and positive in his attitudes, so we let him have another night to run his own club. The kids were keen enough, so he set off, hopes high. We heard rumbles of discontent from the kids after the first week, but Jeff said nothing, so we let him continue.

After six weeks Jeff came to me almost in tears. "I can't do it, Bill," he said. "All I wanted to do was give them a youth club, and the little bastards don't want it." It seemed that, as we had guessed, Jeff had a very short fuse, and kids found this out in about ten minutes, as kids do. They ran him ragged, teasing him, getting him into a temper so he had to close his club early, after he had expelled most of them, who then came round to the windows and tapped on them, just to annoy Jeff. He knew when he was beaten. It was a blow to his pride, and it seemed sad that such a large, well-intentioned man should be unable to do what he had always wanted to do. But there it was, he had not got the temperament for it. He had to give up, and he never came to our club again. But he worked harder than ever for us.

He was a champion fund-raiser. He had some very special knowledge, one of which was how to run a dog show. He suggested doing that, and we all backed off, saying we didn't have any experience, but Jeff was not going to be put off this one. He said he did know, and all we had to do was to do as we were told. So we did. Jeff was brilliant. He knew judges, dog people from all over the Midlands, so we hired the Rugby Club, and just did it. It was hilarious, dog people who looked just like their dogs, the petty squabbles amongst dog people, and the dogs themselves, it was brilliant. We ended up with some lurcher racing, and the gypsies all came for that, betting huge sums on the dogs of their choice. The finale was the terrier racing. A line of Jack Russell terriers are not the best-behaved dogs, and when they were shown the rabbit-skin lure, they went mad. At the off, half of them fell to fighting each other, some tore off into the crowd, some ran backwards looking for their owners, and about two finished the course. We were laughing too much to care who won anyway. When we cashed up that night, we had raised over £1000. We were amazed, but Jeff wasn't.

Jeff and I were an unlikely pair to get along, but we both had something the other wanted and couldn't do. I could run a youth club, Jeff knew everyone and could raise money. We argued about everything. Not so much about the youth club, but about everything else. It was the time of the miner's strike, and Jeff thought they should be shot, and I thought they were right. Jeff called me a Red Commie, and I refrained from calling him a fascist, but only just. I don't think he would have minded much anyway. We had opposing views on almost everything. Country people are strongly conservative, and Jeff was certainly that, with knobs on. But we got along fine, enjoying our arguments. I don't think our long-suffering wives did, though, but they knew better than to interfere. They just gently mocked the pair of us.

Another of Jeff's fund-raising ideas was to have a bodybuilding contest. He knew lots of people who were into serious bodybuilding, including a few women, so we put on a day's show at the Trades & Labour. It was highly successful, but weird. Hugely muscled men paraded before the judges with music playing, and got points for reasons we could not fathom. There was only one woman in the end, but she was the weirdest of them all. Her muscles glistened and rippled like a man's, but I had to admit her performance to the music was full of grace and invention. As the only entrant she won the ladies prize, and she was a charming person, not at all like she looked. I still would not have liked to meet her down a dark alley if she took a dislike to me, though. I met a real-life night-club bouncer too, a giant of six foot eight, who explained to me how you never showed off, just smiled. If there was any violence, he showed me how to immobilise the attacker whilst smiling and looking as if he was just showing him the way out, yet all the time the bloke was in agony from a thumb on a pressure point under his collarbone. He reckoned he could make them faint with pain, and then sympathise with them, since they had no idea of what had happened to them. This was all done so as not to arouse their mates, otherwise all hell would kick off, and the bouncers would lose their bonus. He was a frightening man in his quiet way. Another of Jeff's interesting friends.

Molly came to ask us if she could run a tuck-shop on club night. We jumped at the offer. Molly was Grandma or Auntie to almost half our members, and she knew most of the others as well. She may have looked a kindly old lady, which she was, but she ran that tuck-shop like a pawnbrokers. No kid ever got away with owing even a single penny to Molly. She had an elephantine memory, not just for the money they owed from last month, but what they had said, who was related to who, whose Mum was having it off with whose Dad (although she never let these delicate facts out to the kids themselves), and all the gossip that makes a small town like ours sing. She had a wonderful gift, and she raised us pounds over the years. She would never come to our committee meetings, because she would never go in the Trades & Labour Club, since it was there that her husband had died so many years before. The kids were never rude to her, I suppose because she knew all their parents, and would speak to them if necessary. She was pure gold for our club.

As I was a trustee of the Grogg Hall for a time, we put on the first Rock Concert there. Two bands, one with a young man who was Elcaster born, and a big one from Birmingham. David the manager was very nervous, and I had to work hard to get him to allow it. I told him how much he would make on the bar, how rock fans were mild mannered head bangers, never violent, and how much it would improve the stuffy image of the Grogg Hall. Eventually he weakened, and we put the show on. It was spectacular. The youth club members stood there agape, they had never seen anything like it. The band put on the full show; lights, fog, fireworks, drama, and very loud music. The audience loved it, and their heads were banging fit to bust down at the front. My daughter had just returned that day from Australia, and had drunk four pints of ice-cold lager very fast, and then thrown up over one of the speakers. David came up to me afterwards. "There you are," I said, "Only four glasses broken, and we'll pay for them We made a lot of money for the club."

"No, that's fine, they were very well behaved, as you said. But, you know what? Someone threw up over the speaker. Disgusting, I call it."

"Oh yes, I do so agree, David. I blame the parents,

don't you?"

"Definitely, Bill. No control over themselves."
I never did tell him it was my own daughter who did it.

We put other youngsters' bands on, but always at the Trades & Labour, because the Grogg wanted the money for the hire of the Hall, and the Trades did it for nothing, making their profit on the bar. This was always the attitude of the Grogg, wanting more money than the Trades, so we always went to the Trades. We did discos there, much to the disgust of some of the older members, but the committee welcomed us. The old codgers would complain about the volume, and ask us to ask the DJ to turn it down, so we did. The DJ never changed the volume, he only pretended to, but honour was satisfied on all sides. As their chairman said one night over a pint, "Your youth club members are our future, Bill. Be kind to them now, and they'll repay us in the future." How I wish that the Grogg had taken that attitude too. They were unable to because of their commercial slant, always wanting a profit. They never were a true part of the community, how could they be if they ran it as a business? Who loves a business, especially a grasping one?

We had a lot of fun raising money, and we didn't spend much. We entered a float the Easter Parade for several years running, until the whole parade collapsed from lack of interest in the Town. The kids always did the decorating, and dressed up in the daftest of costumes. Once, it was all we could do to stop them parading naked on our Hawaii beach float. They thought as long as they had masks on, nobody would know who they were.

We didn't do many trips, though. We took them ice-skating in Solihull a few times, and one dreadful evening one of our women volunteers took some to Studley Youth Club, which had a bit of a name for bad behaviour. Lynn, the volunteer, came back quivering, but laughing. I asked her what had happened. 'It was awful, Bill." she said. "Their kids were really nasty, and tried to pick a fight with ours, but they were ever so good, and wouldn't bite. Then one of their little sods flashes at me in the entrance, opens his pants right up."

"So what did you do?"

"I was really scared, but I just came out with it, Bill, I couldn't stop meself."

"Came out with what, Lynn?

"I said, 'Call that a knob? I've had bigger ones that that for breakfast!'"

"Great! And what did he do?"

"He went bright red, pulled his pants together and ran out of the door. I was so scared, though, I was shaking all over!"

"You did the right thing, Lynn. Although you've probably scarred him psychologically for life, he asked for it! Well done! Did you report it?"

"No, I thought he'd had his punishment. Those blokes running their club, they're useless, Bill. The kids were all over the place. We'd have shut it down if it got that bad."

"Maybe. But they were professionals, Lynn. They are

all paid and fully trained in Studley. They can't get volunteers at all."

It was true. Ours was the only club in the whole area running with only volunteers, and from what we saw at other clubs, ours was one of the best-run clubs too.

THE AEROPLANE

This may not appear to have much to do with how to set up and run a youth club. If you think that, you would be right. Few of those who have set up youth clubs will have come across an aeroplane in their travails, probably. On the other hand, how do I know that? I don't even know anyone else besides myself and my friends who have set up a youth club at all, so maybe an aeroplane is an essential ingredient. Whether it is or not doesn't matter. It was important to us at Elcaster as we struggled to get support for our efforts, not so much in the form of money, but in community approval and warm hugs. (There's not many of either in running youth clubs, as you might guess)

The aeroplane had everything to do with the Grogg Community Centre, run at the time by the trustees consisting of Mr Collett the newsagent, his friend Aubrey Gwinnet, and Mr. Dennis Greig, the stockbroker from London. The money from the Grogg shares had been cashed, the Sports Hall was built, a manager was in place, my friend David Rick, when some ugly rumours appeared in some local newspapers. They intimated that the accounts were skew-whiff, and accountants were scurrying to add up the figures, and some were talking to the papers.

Around this same time, when I was working at Aerospace, a charming Polish man came up to me. I knew him slightly, he had been in the Queens Flight as a pilot, so he must have been one of the best in the country, and he had been in the RAF since coming here from Poland at the start of World War 2. He was retired from that now, and working for Lusac Aerospace. One day, he came up to me and prodded me in the chest.

"You live in Elcaster, yes, Bill? That's right, yes?" I agreed it was correct.

"Then you got to do something. You being cheated. These men, they buy a plane, a little one, and they pay me to teach them to fly. They laughing at you in Elcaster, Bill. They say you paying for it all. They treat me like dirt. It is they that are dirt. You come from Elcaster. You got to do something. OK?"

I had read the papers, so I guessed what he was getting at. "All right, Tony. I'll see what I can do."

"You got a son, right? You bring him out to Coventry Airport, to Baggington, next week, yes? Bring a friend of his too. I fly them on your aeroplane. They paid for it. I give them a flight around. You bring them, Bill."

So I did. Tony the Pole gave them a great talk on safety in flying, about never taking risks, not ever, so this is why he's here today. Then he took my son and his friend around the Midlands for half-an-hour in what he called Elcaster's aeroplane. They loved it. So did he. "Now don't forget, Bill. You do something, right?"

I did what I could. The fact that an aeroplane existed was in the local press by now. Denials were made, then it all went quiet. Tony was happy. "They take the aeroplane away, Bill. Was it you did it? They were very scared that last time. I hope I never see them again. Dirt. All of them."

The truth was, I had done nothing. I assumed that the press coverage had been enough to stop whatever was going on, so I thought no more about it. Until we went to visit the Charity Commission, that is.

The trustees at the Grogg Hall had let us alone, but they were acting silly again, over petty rules about who could use the squash club and at what age, stupid little things that nevertheless were contrary to what the Grogg constitution said. So I wrote to the Charity Commission to complain, as the trustees took absolutely no notice of our comments. To my surprise, we were asked to go and see the Charity Commission in person, at their Liverpool office.

Three of us went up. We were shown into an office, and we met the solicitor who would talk to us about our concerns. There was a note-taker in the corner. Jeff got off on the wrong foot by asking the lady solicitor who had paid her off. This was met by a stony silence, but Jeff was only being Jeff.

They started by asking us if we wanted the change in the constitution reversed, so that the Grogg Hall reverted to being a youth club only,which in practice it had never been, instead of a community centre. We said unanimously that we wanted it to stay as it was, provided that special provision was made for young people, and this was to appear in the constitution. The lady agreed, and we went on to our complaints. Luckily, I had evidence for all of them, and could quote chapter and verse; the secretary in the corner was busy writing all this down. We had finished, and the lady asked if we had any more complaints. I said no, then as an afterthought, I asked her if she had heard about the aeroplane.

"Nobody has mentioned it to us," she said.

"It was in the local papers," I said.

"We cannot act upon newspaper reports, only on complaints by beneficiaries of any charity. Tell me about the aeroplane."

So we sat down again, and I told her what I knew, including the fact that my son had flown in it, so I knew it had existed. "But I have no concrete evidence," I said. "Probably the papers didn't get it all right, they never do."

"Can you recall the Polish pilot's name and address? That would help."

"I can't, it was too long ago. Anyway, we have both left the company. I'm sorry"

"Never mind. What you have told me is of great interest. I shall be visiting the Grogg Hall in the future, and I shall notify you, and report on any progress."

She was as good as her word. Six months later, I got a letter asking to meet me at the Grogg, so I did. All our complaints had been put right, and she said so.

"But do not think we have forgotten about the aeroplane. It is just proving more difficult than we thought, but something will happen, and you will know what it is when it happens. Good day, Mr. Bayley"

Six months later, the Chairman of the trustees, Mr. Collett, resigned. He also left the Town, selling his newsagent business. I knew the reason. But nobody else did. Nothing was said by the other trustees. Nothing was said about the money being replaced. Not a word. Nothing appeared in the papers. It was as if Collett had never existed. I told David, the manager, the true reason, and he plainly didn't believe me. The good people of Elcaster went on believing what the papers had said about the aeroplane a few years before, that it had been bought fraudulently by the Grogg trustees. In other words, the chance to put the record straight was lost, and the community thought the Grogg was run by crooks. And since no-one has ever said a word about the truth in public, except myself, they believe that they are crooks to this day, despite not a single trustee of those days being around now.

I believe that the Charity Commission found enough evidence for fraud to go to Dennis Grogg and say "You appointed this man. You get rid of him, and put the money back, or we will drag the name of Grogg through the courts. None of us want that, do we?" The Charity Commission always prefer to act in the silent twilight of anonymity, but act they will, and did.

So that is how an aeroplane affected the provision of a youth club at the Grogg Community Centre. Of course, they realised at the Grogg what mistakes had been made, and welcomed us in, together with the whole community.

I am sadly being ironic. The aeroplane incident only made them meaner and less community minded; in fact, they became paranoid. The new Chairman, a nice man, was simply buried beneath the antisocial history of the place, and he could do nothing to improve matters on his own. Furthermore, he was yet another businessman, and had no real idea about how a community centre should be run. Most of the Townspeople just shrugged their shoulders and said, they're a bunch of crooks at the Grogg. Not a good attitude to grow any community effort.

Our youth club began to have difficulties a year or so after this. The parents who had held it together were losing interest, since their own kids had left, and it was just too hard a job to do any more. They said that the kids had got more difficult, but it wasn't that. They had lost the fire that sustained them in the first years, as most adults do, even teachers. Teenagers are hard to deal with year after year unless you find them endlessly fascinating, and few truly do that. Jeff was losing interest in fund-raising, he had done it for five years, more or less single-handedly, so that was no wonder. Youth clubs are like daffodils, they spring up, bloom, look magnificent, but in their season they die back, wither and disappear. But they have not died. The energy is saved somehow, and they are dormant, to push their way to the surface again when the time is right, and the necessary people have been collected mysteriously together. This is right. It gives the new adults the space to innovate and do it their way without the older ones telling them what won't work. It's always best to find out for yourself. This is why the Youth Service has such a tough time, because. like schools, they have to keep going year on year, with no fallow time. All organisations have a finite life, like any organism, and when it is dying it is best to give it the last rites, move on, and start again. If it was worth doing, somebody will resurrect it, and carry on, but in a new way of their own invention. It does not matter that they repeat all the mistakes, this is how youth clubs work best, with hand-to-mouth vitality and immediacy. Perfection is never attained, nor even closely approached. There is no Perfect Youth Club, no Utopias for Youths. Are there to be youth clubs in Heaven? We shall see if we get there. There are no Etons or Harrows amongst the history of youth clubs, just endless resurgence, the very essence of vigourous life. In their way they are as immortal as the Spring flowers, and nobody says they are done for just because they are sporadic. What a pity that youth clubs are not as welcome as the bluebells!

We tried to keep things going by encouraging the County Youth workers to help, which they did at first. They were jolly young people, full of idealism and energy, but they found Elcaster a hard place to work in. Most of them had been used to City youth clubs, with all the urban attitudes and difficulties, but Elcaster is a rural town, and the young are country lads and lasses. They are cautious, hard to engage until they trust you, lacking in curiosity, hard to get them interested in anything new. The final pair from the County just gave up one night, although they had done their very best, they could not deal with the rudeness and lack of commitment. And that was it. We had not enough adults to run a session, so we called it a day and closed it down. Were we sorry? Later we were, but at the time we were just weary.

STEP SEVEN --- OVERCOMING DIFFICULTIES

"The Tao that is spoken of is not the Eternal nature of the Tao;
That which can be named is not the true Tao"

Tao Te Ching, Chapter 1

It is no wonder that so many kids leave school with few exam passes and bad feelings about education in general. Where they need, and might expect, kindness and encouragement, they find hostility and endless criticism. The kids that are at the bottom of the social heap are the ones we get coming to youth clubs. It is our job to give them what we can of those two qualities, kindness and encouragement. But they certainly make it hard to do so, being often rude, uncivilised and apparently stubbornly unreachable. They are not like that underneath, they are just the same as everyone, if you can find a way to treat them right. Yet finding that way is very hard, and youth workers make many mistakes on the way. They get discouraged and exhausted with the effort, and give up. The way cannot be written down, you will not find it in books or university courses, nor television programmes or instructional videos. The same is true, of course, of many human activities. You cannot learn to paint from a book, yet many think they can, and thousands have earned money by writing books on it. No human activity that requires the participation of the soul can be learned by writing or speaking. If it needs spirit to do, then take courage, jump in, and just do it. You have to really want to do it, of course. When you come across problems, as you will, it is then that words can help you. But even they can only take you so far. Doing it, whatever it is, with others, and talking about it, that will get you onto the way. You will never reach the end, but once you have started truly on the way, you will never want to reach the limit, because there is none. Many activities just need attention, and for them you need instruction, but they do not need any spirit, just a little intelligence. Lots of work is like that now, which is why people dislike it, even as it earns them money to live. But any Art needs the engagement of your soul, and without that engagement you will fail. It will make you miserable, and you have to find something else to do then.

When our first youth club stopped functioning, tiredness was the primary feeling, yet we knew we had done a good job. For me it was a time when I could reflect on what I had done, mistakes I had made, and how I might do it better, if ever I started another one. I thought about the things that had happened, and how, slowly, we had got to know the kids as people.

One event was our week on a barge. There was a 70 foot barge available for youth groups to use, which had been paid for by the staff of Marks and Spencer in Stratford, so we put our name down for a week in August. I had to go on a weekend course run by the barge experts to learn how to handle such a large craft on such a small canal as the Stratford Canal. So I turned up one cold wet March day with about eight other teachers and youth workers of miscellaneous sorts. None of us really wanted to be there, we were all doing it because we wanted to take kids on it, without them falling in too often. We were shown how to work the locks, how to start the diesel engine, how to turn the boat round in the 'winding holes', bits cut into the bank to allow the vast 70 foot length to turn in a canal only about 40 feet wide. We had to do it all on the engine throttle and rudder, and it was not easy. It reduced one junior school teacher to tears, but she got no sympathy from the hard-nosed barge experts, or us, the exhausted pupils. By nightfall we reached a pub, and thankfully fell to eating pub food, drinking and playing darts. Soon the agonies of the day wore off, and we began to enjoy ourselves. I don't remember spending the night on board, but we must have done, and we resumed our trip back to Stratford like old sea-dogs.

We got twelve kids wanting to go on the trip, six boys and six girls. One of the women volunteered to come with us, to look after the girls, but she was not all that keen. So it was no surprise when the girls decided to drop out a week before we were due to set sail. I told the boys, "It makes no difference, we shall still go. You will buy all the food we need the day before we go, and there will be plenty of room on board." They did buy all the food, with help from mothers, thank God, and we went to pick up the boat at Stratford. I was nervous, as it had been months since I had learned all the intricacies of barge control, but the boatyard bloke was great.

"Do you want a brief refresher?" he asked me, sizing up the young crew.

"Oh, yes, please," I cried gratefully. He showed me how to start and stop the engine, where the water was, told me not to worry about the loo, or the gas.

"Actually, it's steering the thing that worries me," I said. He looked at the six lads, waiting to board.

"Nothing easier," he said. "You got six of 'em. Two at the front, two at the side or on land, and two at the back. Use the boat hooks, or just your hand, or foot. Otherwise, its just the rudder, and that's like driving a car."

I could have shaken his hand. What was all that buggering about with the throttle I had been made to do? Just experts making me feel small, justifying their fees, that's what.

The lads stowed all their kit at the prow end, I went to the stern, as far away from them as I could get. We set off with me driving and moored up about half a mile from the boatyard, going towards Birmingham. The other way was the end of the canal where it met the Avon by the Basin on the middle of Stratford. We cooked supper, and I gave them a brief talk on the rules.

"We will not be going to any pubs, and we will not be drinking any alcohol. You will do the cooking, I may take a turn, but you must sort it out amongst yourselves. Likewise with the washing up. In the morning, I will show you all how to steer, how to operate the locks, and you will be in charge of the boat. I shall be sitting in the front, or maybe the back, smoking my pipe if you need me, which I do not think you will, as you all look competent and sensible. One last rule. If, for any two hour period of this week's trip, I am not enjoying myself, we shall turn round at once and go home. Any questions?" There were none.

There being no TV, we all went to bed. I read for an hour, and went to sleep half-hearing the chatter from them all in the front. I think they talked until the small hours of the morning, but I was surprised by a knock on my door around eight.

"How many sugars in your tea, Bill? Breakfast is served." And it was. Bacon and eggs, tea, toast, it was like being in a hotel for me. They washed up without squabbling, and after I had showed them how to start the engine, I lit my pipe in the stern and settled down.

Not for long. We had gone about ten feet when the mooring rope got tangled round the propeller, and the engine stalled. We drifted to the bank and tied up, using the other mooring rope. "Right then lads. I'll show you what has to be done." I lifted the hatch over the propeller, and showed them the rope tightly knotted around the shaft. "You have to untangle that by hand. It is very difficult, and very wet, but unless you do it, we go nowhere. I shall be under that tree with my pipe. Let me know when you have done it. And remember not to let the rope dangle in the water in future."

It took them two hours, but they were pleased with themselves at completing the task. We got under way properly, and soon got to the first lock. I explained the principles, stressing that if you opened both sets of sluice gates at once, the canal would empty, and other people would be very cross indeed with them. They understood perfectly, and soon had a set of roles that they were to perform at every lock we got to. They even timed themselves, to set up a personal record. I just waited and watched in the stern. I was enjoying myself.

It was a perfect holiday for me. The pace of life on a barge slows right down, as the engine will only push the long boat at walking pace. Nobody rushes. The locks are easy to operate, I had a keen crew, and you get time to talk to other boaters. You pass gently through beautiful countryside, and if it rains you go into the cabin. There were no silly 'No Smoking' rules then. For teenagers, there is enough to do at the locks, or fishing, or just mucking about by walking alongside and teasing your mates. There are no shops, no cars, there is not a lot of mischief they can get into, and the constant fresh air makes them hungry and tired. The weather was fine, we had plenty of food, and nowhere particularly to get to. The world was ours.

We stopped near a canal-side pub overnight, and alcohol was not even mentioned. We bought some pub food and sat on the bank in the evening light, just talking and eating. We all went to bed early again, and this time they all went to sleep without delay.

Next day was sunny, some swam in the canal and others got out the tiny inflatable boat and paddled around, laughing a lot. I remembered to check that they could all swim, which they could. We set out again, with me holding the video camera and filming what was going on, both on the boat and on the banks. I wondered vaguely why they were all grinning with suppressed laughter, when I was struck violently on the head, and I fell over. I had hit a branch, and the little sods had seen it coming and let me suffer. I told them I was not enjoying myself at that precise moment, so they sobered up and got me a coffee, recalling my Rule. The radio was playing 'Proud Mary' by Credence Clearwater, very apt as we chugged up the cut towards nowhere. Later we moored up and had supper, and went to bed, after failing to get any picture on the tiny portable TV that someone's Mum had provided.

Every morning without fail the boys got me a cup of tea and cooked my breakfast. They amused themselves in many ways as we sailed, one writing poetry. (He later went to prison for GBH; he was a nice lad, but impulsive). It was about love, as poems always are at his age. Some played cards for money, and many tens of pence were lost and won in frantic spasms of competition.

After the next overnight stop, we decided we would not try to do the Triangle, which was to go to Birmingham, down the canal through Tardebigge, onto the Avon and back up to Stratford. It would take us too long, and mean twelve hours sailing every day. We decided to turn around in the next winding hole and go back the way we had come to Stratford, and go on the Avon from there. So we did that. Nothing could have been easier, we put two on the bank to pull the ropes, one on the tiller and the throttle, to reverse the engine at the right time, and the others scampered about on the boat, along the sides. We did it in about a minute. I remembered how much I had sweated on my training weekend to do it all on the throttle. How pointless.

We moored up again past the pub we had stopped at on the way up, and in the morning the weather had changed. It was raining, and we agreed to make a run for Stratford as fast as we could go. I warned them about getting too cold and wet, but they wanted to get onto the Avon, so we started off. The rain got harder and harder, and they got more and more determined. They took it in turns to go outside to operate the locks, drying off in the cabin before the tiny gas fire after their stint in the rain. They got the rope twisted round the propeller again in their haste, and it took another two hours of pulling and pushing in the rain to get it free, but they did it, without complaint.

We made it to the basin in Stratford by teatime, wet through, exhausted, but victorious, only to find that the river authorities were not allowing any boats out of the canal onto the Avon, because the water level on the river was dangerously high. We had decided to moor in the basin anyway, so it did no matter.

We had hardly spent any money so far, so I said they could go to the cinema and we would get burgers for supper, as we were right beside McDonald's. Off they went, to see 'ET', and I was left to read and think about what we would do if we couldn't get on the Avon.

They came back from the film, and an intense argument started about who had been crying in the film. I said, "Everyone cries in 'ET', it's what you're supposed to do", but it had little effect. Only after they had eaten their beef burgers did the emotions subside. It turned out that they had all cried, but none of them admitted it to their mates.

In the morning, it was still raining, so no chance of a river trip. Someone's Mum and Dad visited, bringing an apple pie and some Bolognese sauce, enough for an army. Then some of their school mates turned up on the quay, and were regally invited in to be given coffee and biscuits, then some more, and soon we were running a small cafe, with guided tours of the boat thrown in. I need not have worried about what we were going to do, they were in their element playing hosts to their mates. In the evening, they were to cook the spaghetti, which they had been out to buy. It turned out they had bought the very fine variety, which stuck together as a ball, and burned slightly. Nothing daunted, they cut it up into sticky lumps and wolfed it down. They had decided to have custard with the apple pie, so they followed the instructions on the packet. The first lot burned, so they did it again. That also burned, and tasted disgusting. So I decided to take a hand, and show them how it should be done. I burned that too. So we went out and bought cream. The pie was wonderful.

We spent the next day, our last, lording it moored up the quay. I lost count of the number of boys and girls who flocked to visit their friends, all of whom had been contacted the day before by phone. More food appeared, brought by parents, who were also shown round after coffee and biscuits, making admiring noises about how neat and tidy it was, how unlike their own bedrooms. They thought it was me that had made them do it, but I had nothing to do with it. It was their own pride in their achievement that was at work.

The next day we had to return the boat to the yard by midday, so we started to tidy up. I say 'we', but I did nothing, except tidy my own cabin. I gave a little speech first. "Look, lads. During the War, I was in command of a battle tank in the desert, and every day old Monty made us polish and sweep every inch of it. If one grain of sand was found, we were on a charge. I want you to do the same. Right? GO!" Later I heard one say, "I didn't know Bill was in the War, did you?" Afterwards, I asked them how old they thought I was. They had no idea, nor did they know how long ago the War was. You can get away with anything if you say it with a straight face.

Of all those six lads, I still see three of them. Two went to prison later, one twice, but later he reformed himself and is an upright citizen today, and complains to me about how different and rude the kids of today are. I agree, nodding wisely, not saying that kids have not changed one jot in my experience. The other went to prison for dealing drugs, much more serious, and as far as I know he is still there, on and off. He was the one who didn't pay up at the end, and the others suggested they went round and 'had a word with him'. He paid in the end, without their doubtless violent intervention. One lad went to Art School and got a degree, but I have lost touch with him. One joined the Army and became a boxing champion. He lives around here, and has kids of his own. The other two were just lads, and made their way as they do. One of them I still see, the other left Town.

I shall never forget that week, though. They behaved as well as any kids can; they were cheerful throughout, no grumbles, few squabbles that I saw, and all of them individually thanked me for taking them. It was a real holiday for me, I said sincerely, no need to thank me. I loved every minute of it.

Once or twice I went camping with the kids of my registration class in the Birmingham Comprehensive where I was a physics teacher. The first time, all the girls came as well as the boys, and we stayed two nights in Inkberrow, watching out for wildlife, ghosts and things to buy (City kids always look out for things to buy, I don't know why). We had a fire on the second night, and we sat around toasting bread and singing songs, pop songs, as well as many from the First World War, like 'Roll out the Barrel', and 'It's a Long Long Way to Tipperary". I asked how they knew them, and they had learned them at Christmas or family parties off their grandparents.

The second time, only the boys came. The girls were charming about it, but they said they were a bit too old to enjoy camping now, so the boys made a list of the food they wanted, bought it, and we set off. There was quite a bit of squabbling about who was to cook the supper, and my colleague and I threatened to go and get fish and chips for ourselves whilst they sorted it out. They did sort it out, and after supper we went to visit my youth club for an hour, as they had asked to do that. There were about fifteen of them, and there were about thirty Alcester kids in the club when we arrived. My city kids trooped into the hut, and stood there in silence, sizing up the situation. The Alcester kids stopped what they were doing, and the two groups gazed at each other for what seemed like hours. There was complete silence. Then one of my City kids stepped forwards and asked for a game of Pool. Then another went over to buy some fizzy drink, and the ice was broken. After another five minutes I couldn't tell who was from where. My City kids didn't want to leave at nine-thirty when we packed up, addresses were exchanged, and it was agreed we had had a good night. When we got back to our camp, they asked to go on a wildlife hunt, so we did, and found a dead badger, waded through a river, got lost (or so they thought), got scared of the silence after midnight, and got back to go to bed and to sleep without much talking, thank goodness.

But now my contact with teenagers was only at the school I taught at, there was no youth club in Elcaster. I didn't miss the youth club much. I had done what I wanted to do, and another group had come along to run a club in their own way. They rightly did not ask us for any advice, because they just had to do it and find out how to get over their mistakes by experience. I was still teaching physics in an East Birmingham comprehensive, with 1600 pupils on two sites. I saw 325 pupils a week, which was ridiculous, but the school was a reasonable one, and the staff did not interfere with each other, and even managed to support each other from time to time, in between their frantic buzzing between classes. So I saw plenty of teenagers, even if they were not local to me, not part of my life as Elcaster kids could be.

I went up to the Trades and Labour club when the new youth club started there, in the main hall one night a week. The older members were far from happy about it, but the man who was in charge, Tony, was getting a large second-hand temporary hut from the Army. They were even going to bring it over and put it up for him. How he did that nobody knew, but Tony was a builder, so perhaps he was calling in a few favours. So the kids milled about and did things like play Pool, table-tennis, darts, as well as annoy adults and make lots of noise. They didn't need my help.

Why did I get more satisfaction out of teaching averagely bright kids basic science, rather than teach bright kids physics? Why did I refuse to teach a Sixth Form A-Level course, when all my colleagues desperately wanted A-Level work above all else? I think it was because of the difficulties involved. To me, anyone can teach bright kids, you just point them in the right direction and off they run. They can learn from the textbook if you are not too good a teacher. But you need skills to teach average kids, and if you don't have those skills, your kids will not do so well. If you do it really well for some, they can go a long way, right up to degree level and into a job, if you can light and tend the fire at first. Clever middle-class kids get a lot of encouragement from parents, relatives, their own friends, so as a teacher you are just one factor amongst many. But with more deprived kids, you may be a very big factor, and for some you are the only one.

Kindness is the key, as it is in animal training. Punishment never works, it engenders fear, and people don't learn properly when they are afraid. They find ways of avoiding your punishments, and then avoiding you and what you have to teach them. The only punishment that works for a short time is the shock of being deprived of your good esteem. Shouting is a good way to show you do not esteem them at that moment, or rather, that you do not esteem what they are doing. You always have to separate the act from the person; "Love the sinner, hate the sin", as the Sally Army used to say. You must not overdo shouting, though, or it loses its impact. You vary the way you do it; speaking very quietly in a menacing voice very close to their ears is also good. The eyes can speak volumes too. You just have to practice and practice and practice, as any actor will tell you.

That is why I love youth clubs. Because I can act like a teacher, with kindness where possible, shouting when necessary (and all the other things mentioned above), with people who are there because they choose to be. They have to be in school, by Law. They can leave a youth club whenever they want to, so if they stay, you must be doing something right. Maybe they enjoy irritating you, being rude to you, testing you in countless ways. If that's what they are doing, you are doing your job as a youth worker. Of course, it is very uncomfortable being on the receiving end of those actions, and you find ways to stop them. But you cannot do it in the way teachers do, by intimidation and punishment, because they will leave, and maybe never come back, or they will react unpleasantly. And it is right that they do that, you are there to interact with them, or what is the point of a club at all? They are your customers, and you have to provide something that they want. They may not value it, because in our blind society, some people measure worth by how much it costs, and most of my youth clubs have been free. But later they know the value of what they had, when they are parents, or talking with their mates in a pub long after they have left the youth club. The value is in the activity itself, and may not be measured in pounds cost, or exams passed, or heads counted. At times, this quality seems imaginary, non-existent, and you wonder why you are doing it at all, without pay, without thanks, without anything you can look at and say "At least I did that." But at other times you know why you do it, except you cannot put it down on paper, nor even talk about it to those who do not do it with you. To paraphrase Shakespeare in 'As You Like It', Corin the shepherd says,

"Sir. I am a true labourer. I earn that I eat, get that I wear, owe no man hate, envy no man's happiness; glad of other men's good, content with my harm; and the greatest of my pride is to see my ewes graze, and my lambs suck."

I could add, "And see my youths play and talk in

kindness and encouragement." It's always the artists who capture the essence of things of the spirit. Did William Shakespeare ever go to a youth club? Probably not one like ours, but he must have done something of the kind, as all those who grow into fully human beings must.

The youth club at the Trades and Labour journeyed its merry way, but after two years they ran short of volunteers, and I and others were asked by Tony to help out. I was missing the rough and tumble of the youth club by this time, so I agreed, along with a young man, Brett. He became the chairman, and we spent many hours talking over what to do in the club. We talked about starting a radio station, Radio Alcester, broadcasting from the top of St. Nicholas' tower. I was joking, but he was serious. Thank goodness, we never got any money to do it.

The County Youth Service had got interested by this time, and a young woman worked there once a week, and seemed to be running it well. She didn't ask for any help, but I was a bit worried about her, being only one amongst so many youths, who could be quite intimidating at times. Before I got involved there had been an incident where the County had sent a young woman over to run the club behind the Greig, and she had been too schoolmarmish with them. They tied her to a chair and danced around, uttering whoops of victory, scaring her half to death. She never came back, and the incident was hushed up, so I wondered if our Vicky was all right.

She was an extrovert, small but tough, and the boys seemed to respect her. There weren't many girls, which I found odd, but youth clubs go through these phases. I spent a couple of evenings with her, and got no sign of anything wrong. The hut suffered from being easy to break into, and stuff was going missing at times, so we didn't leave anything there of value.

Brett phoned me one night and asked me round. It was an emergency, he said. It turned out that the club had hired a video camera for a week or so, and someone had looked at the tape they had made. It was mostly erased, but a tiny bit remained, with images of lads with no shirts on dancing around, clearly smoking large hand-rolled cigarettes, and passing powders to each other. Vicky was clearly involved with them, and was seen snogging more than one of the older lads. It was obvious that the older boys had gained control over Vicky, and had turned the youth club into a Den of Vice. No wonder there had been no girls, it had been mainly older boys that I had seen there, about 16 to 18 years old.

We told Vicky's employer at the County Youth Service that night, and he went round to interview her, with the tape as evidence. She had no option but to admit what had been going on, so she was sacked on the spot. Later, the police told us that they were on to her as a drug dealer, and had followed her to Evesham where she got the drugs for the boys, and were about to arrest her. Thank God for that video tape! The coverage in the papers would have put Elcaster on the map all right, along with the youth club, the youth service, and all of our committee. A narrow squeak.

We advertised for youth workers, as they could not be found in Elcaster for love nor money at that time. It was not, as some suggested, that the parents didn't care about their kids any more. I did some research of my own, and it was mainly that work hours had increased from ten years ago, and men in particular could not guarantee to come on one specific night a week. Teenagers were perceived as more difficult, with the drug scene going, and our experience confirmed that. People were unwilling to get involved in something they had little experience in, where they could get into trouble for touching a kid, and I couldn't really blame them.

We interviewed a married couple from Birmingham, Georgia and Jim. Her mother had come to live here, and they thought that Elcaster would be a good place to work, even though they had to come a long way. They had a lot of experience with city kids, and thought that Elcaster should not prove too difficult. So they began, bringing with them a friend as well, so we got three for the price of two. The County paid them, as they were fully qualified. We had no money to speak of, it had all been spent by Vicky, and there had been no fund-raising events for months.

So we put it around that we wanted younger kids, we

advertised in schools, and slowly some came through the door. Schools are always reluctant to help youth clubs, at least they are in Elcaster, I have no idea why. It might be something to do with the fact that we have their worst pupils, and they think we encourage them to misbehave by being nice to them. I think the attitude of schools is a symptom of what is wrong with them, and why they fail with so many kids, but it didn't concern me much. There were no youth clubs near the school I taught at in Birmingham, otherwise I might have gone. Except I wanted my supper after my thirty-mile journey home, and I didn't fancy hanging around the school for three hours.

Georgia and Jim were great, and I got on really well with them. There were problems, though. We had many more break-ins than we had had before, and this time they were trashing the place, destroying furniture, games, even the fibrous walls. They were getting through the roof, obviously they knew what they were doing. We knew who it was too, it was the older lads we had expelled for drug-taking along with Vicky, but we couldn't catch them. They were getting revenge for spoiling their fun. The police didn't want to know. We could have stopped up all night to get them, but it wasn't worth the effort. Georgia got a steel cage to put inside the hut to protect valuable things like games and computers, but they got into that one night and stole everything inside.

We were all pretty downhearted by all this, and then

Georgia and Jim said they didn't want to go on. "It's just that it's so much harder than we thought, Bill. It's not that they kids are bad, we are used to wicked kids, it's that they don't join in. They don't want to do anything we give to them, they just turn up their noses at anything we suggest. There's no point in us going on, really. We're getting nowhere, and membership is getting lower and lower." She was right, it was. I used to go along when I could to help them out, and I saw what she meant. The place had an air of dereliction, with all the damage done by the break-ins. Georgia and Jim did what they could, but they were tired when they arrived from Brum, after a day's work, and they were city folk, used to city kids. Elcaster was country, although the kids thought of themselves as streetwise, they were country bumpkins compared to the ones Georgia dealt with, and that I taught. Elcaster kids are cautious, wary, not given to displays of unwarranted enthusiasm, more like nocturnal wild animals than the daylight beasts that the city kids resembled.

So we sadly said farewell to Georgia and Jim, which left us without any youth workers. I tried for a bit, and persuaded a friend to try youth work as a challenge. It didn't work. His fuse was too short, and he lost it on the second night. I could see the kids laughing behind his back, and I knew he wasn't going to make it, for the same reason as Jeff years before. He knew it too, and said he had at least tried, which he had, and which was more than lots of people. There were a few women who came in with me, and they were fine, no short fuse problem with any of them. It was just that they didn't enjoy being ragged, acting as policemen, coping with rows, calming tempers, soothing offended teenies; they had better things to do. One went on running a club for the Under Twelves, which continued for ages, and she loved doing it. She and her friends were very good at it too. It was just that when the kids became thirteen, something called puberty happened to them, and they could cope with the girls mostly, but the testosterone atmosphere simply put them off.

The County could produce no workers for us at all. They were not training any either, and the area worker had the gall to tell me that in his opinion, youth work was finished. There was no call for it any more, since Social Services and the Probation Service did the job now. "Where is the kindness, then? Where is the encouragement? Where is the interaction between kids and ordinary adults with no axe to grind? Your brutal government under Mrs. Thatcher wants to destroy the Welfare State! Sod the lot of you!"

It wasn't his fault, of course. I calmed down, but he was only saying what his bosses were forced to say. It wasn't going to get us those youth workers any time soon, though. I struggled on, with a membership of about forty, and an average attendance of twenty, which I could manage on my own. The break-ins went on, but there was nothing to steal, we had little money because we raised none, having few committee members, but we did get a grant from the Town Council. We were grateful, really we were.

One night in November I was there when the electricity supply failed in our area. Most of the kids went home, and about six hung on to see if the lights came back. We had the emergency lights, very dim, and I said, "No, let's not go home. This is just the night to tell ghost stories."

"Do you know any, Bill?"

"Do I know any! Do you know about the Giant Elcaster Gibbet?"

"What's a gibbet?"

"It's a gallows, where you hang criminals. And the Giant one is buried........... right below where you are sitting now!"

The atmosphere was perfect, so speaking in a very low voice, I made up the story as I went along.

THE GIANT GIBBET OF CROOKES LANE.

No-one has ever heard the whole story until now. At least, no-one who has not met a violent and agonising end. Are you sure you want to hear it, knowing that? All right, I'll tell you. I should think the danger has gone, since you took no part in the ghastly events anyway.

You know why Crookes lane is so named? No, not because of who lives there now, it was named after the family of hunchbacks who lived there for generation after generation, and the Town hangman was always one of that family. They were much feared and respected in their way, because there was no doubt that they were good at their job. The gibbet stood at the junction of Crookes Lane and the

Great Alne Road, and in those days it was at the edge of that stretch of dark and foreboding woodland that was the Forest of Arden. Wolves, bears, all manner of strange beasts dwelt secretly in its depths, and it sheltered many a band of thieves and brigands too. They were not like Robin Hood, they were far from merry. Throats were slit for a groat, and when they were caught, they were tried and sentenced the same day. More work for the Crookes. The bodies were hung in chains, and left swinging in the wind, until the next one arrived, when the rotten carcass was flung to the local dogs.

The land around Gunnings Bridge was marshy and foetid, and only a few outcasts lived there, the Crookes amongst them. Some time in the Middle Ages the Town decided to put up a new gibbet, and it was to be the largest one ever seen, the biggest in the land. The local Duke had married, and the townspeople thought there would be no better way of showing their respect for the Law that the Duke embodied than to put up this huge scaffold, capable of taking six men at a time. It was duly erected after much searching for the right oak, and it was ready for its first use.

It did not have long to wait. There was a spate of weird murders one January, around the time of the full moon, and no-one was caught, but there were rumours abounding. Some said 'Werewolves', some said 'vampires',some said it was the work of Satan. In February they came again, also at full moon, terrible deaths. A search party found a man hiding in the forest, covered in blood, and when he was examined, they found he had an animal-like pelt. A drawing of him exists in the Black Room at Warwick Castle, but no-one is allowed to see it now.

He was tried and sentenced in a matter of minutes, and passed to the Crooke family for swift dispatch. Later that day, the grandmother Crooke appeared in front of the Mayor, saying she would not allow her family to hang that 'thing'. In vain, the Court Leet pointed out is was the Crooke's job, no-one else knew the arcane secrets of the executioner's trade, but she was adamant. The job was given to a colossus of a man, Art Trumble, a bit simple but very strong. So Art went with the Leet and all the Townspeople, who had heard of the trouble by this time, to the lockup in the Town Hall. The criminal was hauled out, and pushed, pulled and manhandled to the new gibbet. Art Trumble lifted him up bodily, put the noose around his neck, and stood him on the cart ready for the final drop. He was asked if he had any last words, and then he started to speak.

His voice was unlike anything heard by man before. It sounded black and poisonous. He spat out the most terrible curse upon those present, upon the Town of Alcester, and upon any that should disturb his grave. In a panic, the Mayor gave the sign to whip the horses. Poor Art mistook it and fell under the wheels. He was crushed to death at the same instant that the murderer's neck was jerked by the noose.

Even then, it took him hours to die. No-one could bear to watch, except some daring lads who stared from behind a hedge, until they passed out in a faint. Later, they could not say what had happened, and they were all touched in the wits from that day onwards.

When the Townsfolk dared to approach the now-silent

corpse swinging there on the edge of the marsh, they were dismayed to find their new gibbet cracked right down the middle, useless for its purpose now. They chopped it down and buried it, along with the terrible thing hanging on it, under ten feet of Warwickshire soil. They forgot about it in time, and put up another scaffold on the Stratford Road, a much healthier place for such a thing, or so they said.

They forgot it, that is, until they came to build this Youth Club, back in the 1980s. When they were digging the foundations, the three men working the mechanical digger found a sliver of black wood in the bucket. Peering into the hole, they saw a gleam of white. One jumped in and showed the others the bone he had discovered. They all leaped into the trench, and had soon uncovered the complete skeleton. Complete, that is, but without a head. Two of them wanted to fetch the police, but one was keen to find the skull, as he thought it might have gold teeth. They searched until dusk, then gave up and returned to the digger.

As the driver opened the door, he felt all the hair on the back of his head stand up. His eyes were fixed on the terrible thing on the seat of his machine. It was the skull all right. Its teeth were not gold -- they were stained with blood. Fresh blood.

Well, you probably know the rest of the tale. The police came, declared it to be a very old corpse, and the Warwick Museum sent an archaeologist, who declared it to be what I have told you, the giant gibbet and its last and only victim. But what few know is that the Church refused to have anything to do with it, so the skeleton was buried where it was found, here, under this Youth Club. And so was the skeleton, although that is a dark secret, so don't spread it.

You probably know how the digger crew had that terrible accident the following month on the Motorway site, being buried for days under mountains of soil, poor fellows. None of them survived. It's not a job for the soft, is digger-driving. Especially in ancient graveyards. So let's hope this Youth Club stands for Eternity, and that monster's grave lies undisturbed in future, because it seems that the curse is still alive.

(That Youth Club was burned down in the 1990s, but no excavations were carried out on the site. Yet)

At the end of this story, there was a silence. You could hear the wind breathe, and something squeaked. The lights were still off. I said to the fourteen-year-olds, "Well, time to be going home then."

One of them said, in a tiny voice, "Could you walk us back, please, Bill?" Of course I would.

For weeks after that I got kids begging me to tell them the story of the Giant Gibbet. I couldn't remember it really, so I wrote it down. Then I wrote another, and another. Then I published 'The Little Book of Elcaster Ghosts". I sold over 120 on the book-signing night. It's still 'in print', if you want a copy. Just ask me. My wife says I should go making up ghost stories and selling them, people will think they're true. How do you know they're not? I ask. Maybe instead of appearing to me in the twilight, they revealed themselves in my mind, just as I was sitting at my word processor. Ghosts are strange creatures, they don't go by the usual rules at all.

STEP EIGHT --- STAYING WITH IT

WHY OUR YOUNGSTERS ARE FEARED

I have been running a drawing group at Age Concern, and when they found I was involved with the local Youth Club, some of them told me stories about our members that made my toes curl.

One lady, who uses a stick, told me that about six of them had surrounded her car when she was shopping in the local precinct, and bounced it up and down as she was trying to get into it. Appealing to some adults nearby for help, she was told that they were as scared of them as she was. They continued to jeer and mock her as she drove away. The same lady told me that about twenty of them had come round to her house and destroyed the water meter, quite gratuitously. She called the police, who told her that it was a matter for the Water Board, and anyway, by the time they would have got round to her house, the kids would have gone, so they did nothing. The Water Board came the next day and fitted a new meter.

Another elderly lady told me how the kids outside a shop in the precinct had pushed each other in her path, and laughed when she tried to tell them off. Again, no adults came to her aid, fearing reprisals from the youngsters, and being charged with assault by the police.

Two of the ladies told me of 'knocking and running' incidents very late at night (after 10 pm), done by large groups of kids making a great deal of noise amongst themselves as they did so. They were both afraid to go out, as in the past they had been sworn at and physically threatened by the kids using aggressive gestures.

Out of the ten old people in my group, all of them had some story to tell of abuse and mockery by kids around the shopping precinct. None of them had made any attempt to engage with the youngsters, as they had past experience that told them that it merely escalated the abusive behaviour. Only one, a man, told me of some help he had had from other adults. All were frightened to go there to shop after dark now, and none of them had a good word to say about the kids they encountered there.

About half of them had stories to tell about how pleasant some young people could be at times, even ones they did not know, but the prevalent attitude from this group was that the kids were out of the control of parents, the police would do nothing to help, and that other adults were as frightened as they were.

My own experience there is different. I usually know one or more of the teenagers, and am able to engage them in conversation, but they can be loud and rude to me, in which case I can be loud and rude back. Usually they are showing off to their friends, mostly other boys, but sometimes girls. Girls are less prone to be rude, but the old people in my group told me that the girls could be worse than the boys, using fouler language and sometimes threatening violence.

I have had many incidents of knocking at my door, and I always take some action, usually opening it quickly and identifying the kids responsible. I have had to threaten one boy with police action, which had no immediate effect, but he did stop doing it a week or so later. I am not frightened of them because I know them, but my wife is. Often their motive

is mischief and to mildly annoy, but they are unaware of the terror that their actions can engender when the old people concerned do not know them, and have their heads filled with stories from the media of violence. Even when I have tried to explain to some of these youngsters how frightened old people become, they are mocking and scornful, plainly believing that old people are wimps and deserve what they get. There is an almost total lack of empathy. I would like to find an old person brave enough to come down to the Youth Hut and talk to them, but none of those I spoke to wanted to go anywhere near them.
I suspect that I was not told all the details by the old people, particularly of what might have led up to the incidents. There is a lot of misunderstanding about how the generations speak to each other, but I have no doubt that the kids were bullying the elderly when they saw they were afraid and unlikely to make an effective response.

I have a few ideas about how to tackle this problem, but this is not the place to go into them. It would take time and some intermediaries to get the two sides together, but it could be done, and should be initiated by the Youth Service. Plainly, the police are not interested or competent, and the old people have no organisation to turn to, which is a shame. *(Bear Flag, October 2001)*

This was a fair summary of the situation in some parts

of the Town, and for all I know it still is. I do not know what has happened between the generations. I could hazard a few guesses, but they would only be from my own experience, and without the force of wide statistics. All I can do is to plod on, talking to both sides, hoping that some of what I may say to both could rub off and affect behaviour. It is clearly useless to rely on the Government to do anything, or any authority, as they are powerless at the local level. We simply have to work something out amongst us, but who will take the initiative? Who will make a start?

I suppose the old people might have done better to play the young yobs at their own game, and ganged up on them, but oldies have lost the knack of forming gangs. They should have joined the Geriatric Youth Club. This mythical club has been going hypothetically for about twenty years, since I invented it. The fictitious members are people who were in the Army, at boarding school (like me), or just too busy or scared to join a youth club when they were younger. Their motto is , "Divided we fall, together we can bugger about until we die." Our aims are diverse, but they are mainly to be a nuisance to young people, and shout at them rudely when they are crossing the road, to refuse to bow to any authority, to refuse to conform to any old-age stereotype, and to have a good time regardless of what others think of us. We are now old enough to do most of these things. Membership is open to all over 60, male and female, and our efforts to hold an annual dinner have failed repeatedly, since no-one will tolerate our behaviour when drunk. Or sober, for that matter. many have been called to a Higher Club in the Sky, but we still recruit from the ranks of the newly-retired. Some people actually believe that the Geriatric Youth Club, really exists. Maybe it will, later.

Many of those who complained about the behaviour of young people in the above article think the Geriatric Youth Club is merely a joke, so they can only get token support from us. All they would have to do is recognise our validity, and we could spring into action, and pit our gangs against the kid's gangs. But while they remain intransigently alone and refuse to join up together, they are condemned to rely on the protection of other adults and the police, and you can read above how ineffective those are.

Two years or so before I found myself one of two adults trying to keep the youth club at the Trades together, I had retired from full-time teaching in Birmingham. The events that led to it are farcical, which was no surprise, since Birmingham Education Department were by far the worst employer I ever had. It was probably not entirely their fault, as money had been stolen blatantly from Education by the Socialists on the Council to fund irresponsible nonsenses like the Ring Road, to the glory of Socialism. As a consequence, the Education Authority, once the best in the country in the 1960s became grossly underfunded, and frankly, a laughing stock. This was reflected in the fact that thousands of Birmingham kids had an appallingly scant education, except for the lucky few who went to the King Edward schools. The great comprehensives, once the models on which others were based, became bloated, understaffed and run-down, at great cost to the pupils. The one I taught at for five years was 1600 pupils 'strong', with classes of over 35, and managed by as big a bunch of fools as I had even met in industry, which is saying something. The kids themselves were fine, and so were their parents who almost universally loved them. Why did they not rise up and complain vigourously about the rotten deal they were getting? Because Birmingham people were respectful of authority, and always believed they were doing their best. It made me weep with frustration to see how they would meekly take the latest cuts, tolerate rank teachers, and never lay any blame at the door of those responsible, the Council and the Government of the day. I had a reasonably good time at the school, mainly because I had learned to ignore the management, and just get on with teaching inside my kingdom, the classroom, where they couldn't touch you as long as you delivered the goods; content pupils and parents, and adequate exam results.

When my friend Rob told me they were looking for older teachers to retire early, I assumed I would not get a look in, as they were advertising for new physics teachers at that time. But Rob worked closer to the feeble heart of the Authority, and he told me that those making the redundancies were at daggers drawn with the recruiters, and I should put in my application. I had to get the Head's approval, but we had a hearty mutual dislike, so I wrote that strange letter, the application for redundancy.

It was the mirror image of a letter of application. I had to convince them how bad I was at the job, and likely to get rapidly worse. I had to say what a liability I might become in later times, and how overwhelmed I was by all the new advances in education they were bringing in, to the benefit of the pupils, needless to say. It was a monument of hypocrisy and downright lies, and I was very proud of it. Rob thought it would do, and so it did. They even gave me an extra seven years pensionable rights as an inducement. I would have gone without that, but to this day I get £200 a month from Birmingham, as a memorial to what stinkers they were. I intend to live to be 120, just to keep taking it.

My mother was indignant. "You can't retire at 51! It's not natural!"

"Just watch me, mother. My Uncle Derek retired at 45, and you didn't tell him it was unnatural."

"No, but he worked in Africa, and he wasn't married. That's different."

"Can't see it, mother. Anyway, it's no business of yours. It will mean I can come and see you more often, maybe." I regretted that promise later when she tried to keep me to it, but I relied on the phrases 'more often' and 'maybe' to shelter me. Possibly I should have been a lawyer, as my mother said.

I did have a twinge of worry before I accepted. Would we manage in the reduced income? Would I get depressed and sit at home all day? What would I do to occupy myself? I would lose all my holidays, since every day would be a holiday. My wife made up my mind for me. "If you don't accept it, never again complain to me about work." That did it. She didn't mind having less money. I accepted.

I had to go on a course run by my employers, for teachers who were retiring. Most of us were mid-fifties, and full of life and vigour, barely able to believe our good luck. It was fun, because none of us took it seriously, none of us were remotely old. We were lectured about health, and shown exercises to do whilst sitting in an armchair. We were talked to about starting our own businesses, and we were warned to do Market Research before we invested all our pension. Asking the man if he knew anyone who did market research, he had to say he didn't know. A fat lot of good he was, then. We had a presentation from an investment company, which looked good, except all my lump sum was spent in my head, on a BMW motorbike, or perhaps a Honda Gold Wing. Later, that company were sued by a group of teachers for mis-selling. Trust Birmingham Education to pick the wrong one. I am slightly ashamed to say we behaved quite badly during that retirement course, irritating the lecturers and generally mucking about like naughty schoolchildren, of which we had had enormous experience. The women were as bad as we men, and we didn't feel in the slightest way sorry for the teachers. We were free, and we relished the feeling.

Finally, I had an interview with their Personnel department, to tell me my prospects. A power-dressed lady sat me down, and said, "You are lucky, Mr. Bayley. Where you live, you have access to many Education Authorities, Warwickshire, Gloucestershire, Worcestershire, Solihull, and you can work half-time in any of them without your pension being affected. You can work any amount of time you want in private schools. But I have to tell you that you will not be allowed to come back to teach in Birmingham, I'm afraid."

"Madam, I have no intention of ever setting foot in your benighted, incompetent, dismal little excuse for an Education Department ever again, in this life, the next, nor any I may have in future."

She looked at me wistfully, her eyes showing me how much she envied me. "I know how you feel," she said sorrowfully. The interview was at an end. I heard her sigh as I left the room, my head high and my heart eager for the future life of doing nothing and getting paid for it.

We went on holiday to Ireland that summer, after saying farewell without a single regret to my colleagues. I had to enter my 'profession' in the immigration form. It felt strange when I wrote, "Retired Teacher". I didn't feel in the least retired. I would miss the kids, I knew that, but I had the youth club, and maybe I would get a job somewhere. No hurry, though. I wanted to get the feeling of not working, and I had all the time in the world.

The best day was the first day of term, when my wife went back to work, and I stayed at home, without a single pang of regret, only joy at my release. I had been waiting all my working life for this magical moment. Work had never really suited me. I had too many things to do. I should have done this years ago. I decided to teach myself to paint in water-colours, so I forced myself to sit down every weekday by 9.30, and get on with my task, for at least four hours a day. I was more strict with myself than any employer had ever been. I thought it would take six months, It took two years before I was happy with the results, but long before then I had taken a job. Then two jobs. But I gave it six months before I did anything except paint.

My first job was in a private school, one owned by my friend David. It was in Solihull, and took pupils up to eleven. He wanted me to teach science to his Year Six, one afternoon a week. I would never have worked in a private school in my working career, but now that was over, I thought it might be interesting. I made some conditions: One, I did not have to meet the parents, Two, that I set no homework. Three, he bought me any equipment I needed, within reason. These were readily agreed by David, who thought I might annoy his parents anyway, and the kids had enough homework already. He bought everything I asked him to, always. How different from State schools! We agreed a rate to cover my travel from Elcaster, and I started.

I knew David's principles when employing staff. First, they had to be competent, and not ask him what to do. Second, they had to fit in with his existing staff, and not upset them. I thought these were sound principles, but when

I was met by the Deputy Head, she told me I was the only man in the staff room, and I was not to sit and pontificate like the last man they had had. I was not informed what she meant by 'pontificating', so I was anxious as I went in. There were about fifteen middle-aged ladies, who turned and looked me up and down, as only junior-school teachers can. I sat in the corner and refrained as hard as knew how from 'pontificating'. I said nothing for at least ten minutes. When I ventured an opinion, they laughed very nicely, which is what they were supposed to do, as I had tried to be funny. A little voice told me, "Don't let it go to your head, Bill. Shut up now", so I did.

I got on so well that the other teachers wanted me to teach their pupils science as well, as it gave them an hour off. So I ended in teaching for the whole day, down to the seven-year-olds, of whom I was rather nervous. Their teacher said to me one day, "You know, Bill, they are getting away with murder with you, they've got you wrapped round their little fingers." I thought about what she had said, and tried being stricter and making them work a bit harder. Sure enough, she was right, the little toads. It just taught me that there is little difference between teaching eighteen-year-olds right down to seven-year-olds, they are all pretty much the same, except for the words you can use.

I found teaching those kids lovely, with no discipline problems at all. In fact, I was a bit bored at times, so I went round stirring up trouble, just to give me something to do. I had no laboratory, but I was used to that from my State school days of ill-equipped classrooms, so I devised lots of practicals using only a desktop. We used spirit burners, later candles, and did a full range of chemistry, physics and biology. I had a lot of fun there, with complete freedom to do what I thought right. It was not what I was used to.

The staff room turned out to be a complete delight. Once they had realised that I was not going to trot off to David and tell him what they were saying, they treated me very well. They loved to argue, and put me down mockingly as 'just like a man'. I had to put a notice in my equipment cupboard, warning about 'sexual molestation of elderly gentlemen.' The kids asked about it when they saw it, and I had to be careful what I said. From time to time the women would want to talk to each other about Women's Problems, and I used to be told to 'go down the other end of the table, Bill, and shut your ears.' I went, but listened intently. I was amazed. I had no idea that women found sex so funny. Their husbands would have died of shame if they knew what I heard at the end of the table. It was a real education for me.

Later, I offered to teach Technology as well as Science, for an extra day. I would do balsa wood modelling, Technic Lego, and video making. I needed the whole day, rather than have to put the stuff away constantly. David agreed, and the staff were delighted. It meant a whole day off for them every four or five weeks. The kids responded well, especially to the video-making. They were allowed to do what they wanted, as long as it took place in the room, they wrote a story-board, and I worked the camera. They performed in groups, or the whole class, or individually, it was their choice. I always left 20 minutes at the end to watch what they had done. They wanted to show their parents at Open Days, so I agreed, even though it meant breaking my vow not to meet any of them. They were universally pleasant; I need not have worried.

The job had grown into two days, and I was still being paid at the rate I had negotiated for one afternoon. This meant I was getting almost as much for my two days as the other teachers were getting for a whole week. I knew this would lead to trouble eventually, so I told David I had to talk to him about pay. He avoided it for weeks, but I pinned him down and asked what other part-time teachers were getting. He told me, and I settled for the same amount. I had never had to negotiate a pay drop before, but it was only sensible. I didn't want things here to go wrong, I enjoyed it too much. It was not work at all, not as I had known it.

I also got another job at the beginning of the new academic year. St. Benny's, the Catholic Sec. Mod. wanted me to teach science part-time, so I agreed some conditions. First, they would give me unpaid leave whenever I wanted it. Two, I would only teach Years Ten and Eleven, the exam years. I was fed up with the Government's pathetic schemes for Science in the early Secondary years, and teaching to exams was what I liked. Third, I would do no training days if I didn't want to. The Head, Tim, agreed to all of them, which was unusual, so it meant they really wanted me. So I started back at a State School, for the maximum, two and a half days. This meant I was now teaching four and a half days out of five. I had Friday afternoon off. But neither job was like work used to be. In any case, I could always leave if I wanted, without losing a big fraction of my pay. In fact, I did leave St. Bens after a year, because I found it too difficult to work with my Head of Department. He insisted that I crossed the t's and dotted the i's in meticulous detail over the exam work, and I refused, as it was unnecessary.

"What's the blasted point, John? Nobody will ever know that I haven't assessed them by a test. It's only a guess, after all."

"I am Head of Department, Bill. My reputation is at stake."

I was astounded. His 'reputation' was non-existent, as a teacher. Kids ran rings round him. He meant his reputation as a bureaucrat, I assumed. So when the Deputy Head asked me what I would do the next term, I said, "Nothing. I cannot work with John any more. He is too fussy about his paperwork, and not enough about his teaching. I am the other way inclined." A bit pompous, but I had to say it.

The next term the poor man had a breakdown, and I was asked if I would go back, and of course I did. He never returned, and was retired sick. I got on famously with his replacement, a Goth called Miss Tara, a young woman who could terrify the kids, "because she's scary." She could cut a naughty pupil to pieces with her sarcastic tongue when she wanted, which was very rarely, but she had no discipline problems at all. She was a great teacher.

Back to the youth club. The club at the Trades was running spasmodically, with some help from me, when I heard a rumour through the grapevine. Now the grapevine in our Town is a sturdy plant, with many branches, twigs, and offshoots. The Rector told me that a man with money from a Trust fund wanted to put some of it into Elcaster, not in a youth club, but in some other way. I asked around as to who this person might be, and got nowhere. I was mildly complaining to an acquaintance of mine in the Three Tuns, when he said, "It's me, Bill." I didn't take it in at first, and went on gently whinging, and he repeated it.

"What do you mean, Stanley, "It's me". What's you?"

"The bloke you're talking about. The rich bastard with all the talk and no do, it's me. I'm the rich bastard."

"Oh." I was stuck for words all of a sudden.

"My wife and I are trustees of this fund that my uncle left, and we have to give money for young people in the area. We gave it to the County Youth Service once, and they paid one of their deadheads to sit in Church House for a year and do absolutely sod all. So I'm not giving it to them again. I actually contacted your Rector, but he hasn't come back to me yet. Have you any ideas, apart from your youth club?"

Yes, I said, I have. Leave it with me. So I rang the Rector, who had already contacted some of his Holy pals. He invited me to a meeting with him and his chums, and the Four Vicars and Me committee was set up.

It was plain that two of them had mentally earmarked the money for one of their own God-bothering schemes. The Rector was neutral, with no ideas of his own, and the other one liked the idea of doing something secular. So we talked and we talked, and someone asked, "What do the youth of the Elcaster area actually want? Or need?"

I had an idea. "I know a chap who can do some research into that. He is a qualified teacher with a lot of experience in social psychology, and he could find out for us. He would need paying, though. He doesn't do anything for free."

I was thinking of my mate Rob, who had retired a year after me, and would welcome a little cash to do what he used to do in Birmingham for the Education Authority. Our Rector said he would not bother the rich Stanley, but he thought he could get about £500 from a local Charity fund to cover it.

Rob did his research for £500, and came up with an excellent report called "Who needs money?". The gist of it was that money alone would do nothing without someone with ideas to use the money productively. So at the next Four vicars and Me meeting, Rob came along, and we agreed that we should use Stanley's money to pay a co-ordinator to promote youth projects in the area, for a fee of £10,000 a year. And yes, Rob was interested in doing it.

We went to Stanley, who had read the report, and he agreed to give us the money, for one year. We were in contact with a retired Chief Inspector of Police in Stratford, who had ambitions to reduce youth crime in the area, and we were asked to go and see him for a meeting, with councillors and other representatives of youth organisations, like the Youth Service.

So along I went with two formidable ladies, one the current Elcaster Mayoress and the other the ex-Mayoress. We sat around a large table in Stratford with all these important people. We had got the money from Stanley, and we were only there out of politeness, to keep the others informed.

Hot air streamed to and fro, blather piled up in heaps, and I was getting fed up rapidly. I put our ideas out to the assembly, and it was well received by most, except the Youth Service man, who tried to tell me how much we needed him and his organisation. I was particularly fed up with him because he didn't like Elcaster, and was failing to provide us with a properly staffed youth club, so I told him straight.

"Mr. Edwards, we don't need you, we have out own funding. When we need you, we will ask for you, and you will give us help in ways we ask for, not in ways you think necessary."

He exploded like an over-shaken pop bottle. He called

me a 'dinosaur', with an 'attitude like in the 1950s', and other names he thought would diminish me. I sat and smiled. "Have you finished, Mr. Edwards? Yes? I think we have said all we need to say here. We shall just get on with what we have to do."

On the way back the two Mayoresses were chortling. "You put him in his place all right, Bill," one said. "Pompous little prick." Such language, and from a Civic dignitary too. But she was right.

We formed a committee full of worthies, more than we wanted, since one we had invited to join went around inviting others. I thought that was a damn cheek, but Rob said, let it ride, we can deal with them.

The first committee meeting was exciting. We had about five members who fitted the requirements of the constitution, which I had written, with Rob's help. I had not discussed it with the others, since we were not a committee then. One particular condition was that no-one could join as a representative, they had to live in the area and be concerned in some way with youth. No other conditions were permitted, although the 'youth' thing could extend to anyone we wanted, like parents. But I certainly did not want representatives who came along to speak up for their organisation, and had little commitment to the EYP and what we were trying to do. I wanted no people like the obnoxious Mr. Edwards. I had had a bellyful of those people when I was working, they are jobsworths, self-importantly there to protect their jobs and tick their own career boxes. So when a notoriously dull bureaucrat from the Youth Service turned up expecting to join, I took some delight in telling him the truth.

"But I have been asked to join!" he said.

"Not by me you haven't."

"Yes, by Councillor Jones. She asked me to come."

"She had no business doing that. This is not her committee. I shall have a word with her later. Now, Mike, you're welcome to a coffee before you go."

"So there's nothing I can do?"

"No, nothing at all. You see, you do not live in the area, and we don't allow representatives on this committee. That is in our Constitution. I know, because I wrote it. Good bye."

"Edwards said you would be trouble."

"Yes, I am. He is perfectly correct. Trouble for him alone, though, and all jobsworths. Now, cheerio, Mike. See you in our non-existent youth club, no doubt."

"Do you mean I am a jobsworth?"

"Not in the least, but if the cap fits... Bye."

I am not ashamed to say I really enjoyed doing that. Councillor Jones was very wary of me from then on, as well she might be. Her heart was in the right place, but she was a died-in-the-wool bureaucrat, but with useful contacts, so we could use her. But she was not going to use us.

We had to advertise the post of Co-ordinator, and hold interviews. We had six applicants, some of which were unsuitable, some who lived outside our area, and we narrowed it down to two. The Grammar School head was now on our committee, and clearly fancied himself as the main interviewer. I decided that was not a good idea, so we had a panel; him, me and one of the others. At the last minute, one of the two cried off, leaving only Rob in the field. The Headmaster plainly thought we had fixed this to get Rob the post, so in the interview (which he insisted must go ahead) he was quite abrasive to Rob. This was meat and drink to Rob, who was well used to dealing with pomposity, and so he did. I could barely keep a straight face at times.

"So, Mr. Mount, why do you think you are suitable for this post?"

"I have experience, and above all a moderate amount of humility. I am extremely proud of my humility."

I turned away to stifle my laughter. Rob got the job, but the head was suspicious of him from that moment on. He must have picked up that Rob was laughing at him, since neither of us had any respect for Headmasters, and although he had veto powers in his school, here he was just one of about seven committee members. He just wanted to look good, and resented our disrespect. Too bad.

I will not set down all the things we did on that committee, as the EYP, but we had a lot of fun. It was harder to get things off the ground, and Rob had to put in a lot of hours on some of our projects, but we were proud of what we did. There was the Skate Park, involving a group of kids who detailed what they wanted, even building a model. We sent many kids on trips, to foreign parts, on yachts, in groups. We had public meetings to tell people what we were doing. We started active groups, such as the writing group (which also involved older people). We tried to start a Town cafe for young people in the evening, but they didn't come in any numbers. I spent six weeks every Tuesday sitting in a cafe waiting for kids. The most we ever had was fourteen, so we had to pull the plug on that. We even lent our hut at the Greig to young bands for practising.

The hut at the Greig was a concession from the Greig trustees towards a youth club. We paid a rent, of course, but at least they had let us in. maybe it was easy for them, since we were all adults, and not likely to misbehave. But at least they did something.

We were so successful that Stanley gave us another £10,000 for a second year. He was quite brilliant, he never asked for a report, although Rob produced one every three months. He never checked on what we were doing, never quibbled with us, he just let us get on with what we knew we could do. A pity that other funders do not do likewise, instead of interfering in things they know nothing about. The government are worst of all; if they give you money, they assume they have bought your soul. This is why so many things fail, of course. Only trust will produce the goods, trust and a little common sense to see when you are being ripped off. Without trust, people will not do their very utmost; why should they? How can you respect someone who does not trust you? This was a theme in Rob's paper, "Who Needs Money?", and it is more valid today that it was then.

During our second year, the youth club collapsed. Slowly but inevitably, kids stopped coming, since there was no leader, and only intermittent volunteers. The County showed no interest, even though there were County-funded clubs in all the small Towns around, Henley, Studley, Bidford, and of course, Stratford. Eventually there was no point in opening, and there were only two committee members left, and old Town Councillor and me. We agreed, what was the point of two grandfathers trying to continue to get support, when neither the kids nor their parents were coming through the doors? The building was still costing us £1000 a year, so we gave it to the Town Football Club, who had 200 youngsters on their books. After only a year, the Elcaster Arsonist burned it to the ground. He had settled the hash of the Cadet Hut earlier, but they got a brand new hut from the War Office, behind the Greig Hall. Nobody would rebuild a youth club, and the footballers could easily do without it, so it went into Paradise unmourned. An era had ended. There was no youth club in the Town at all now.

Except one. There was a youth club run by church women, from St. Nicholas', and it was all girls. No, there was one heroic boy. You might think he was lucky, but he had a very hard row to hoe, to keep up his masculinity in the face of all that ferocious femininity, but he did it somehow. I was asked to go there and do some video work, or drama, or whatever the girls said they wanted. It was a little daunting, because it was so unlike any youth club I had ever gone into. For a start, it was quiet. Then I was greeted properly by a few girls, introduced to others, and asked if I wanted a cup of tea. Usually when I go into a youth club, at best I am ignored, at worst I am insulted in some non-subtle way. Occasionally the harassed adults will ask if you are all right, but the kids treat you as an intruder, mostly. So this feminine hospitality was welcome but unsettling. I wondered when they would yell "Suckerrrr!", and run round me screaming.

I asked them what they wanted to do, and they said it was up to me, whatever I felt most comfortable with doing. So I got out the video camera, and explained the rules of the Family Therapy Improvisation. One tall girl volunteered to start. When I asked her who she wanted to be, she said a New York gangster. This threw me a bit, since my own rule is that I have to let the kids choose their characters, and I must not interfere. She went on, told me about her drug habit, and she picked her dealer. She in turn picked the rival gang boss, and so on.

The video started with a massacre, with girls dying startlingly realistic deaths, and then coming back to life as ghosts. I lost track of the plot early on, but they didn't. There were murders, police raids, bombs, everything you could imagine from the most violent X-rated movies. They loved it, and they laughed and laughed when they watched it later. The adults, mostly mothers of the girls, looked slightly shocked, but didn't say so. I realised that the girls were mostly from Elcaster Grammar School, had been doing Drama as a subject, and were just letting their hair down.

Why were all these girls at this youth club, who would never be seen in any of my youth clubs,and why were there no kids here from the High School either? You don't need to be too clever to work it out. It's about meeting with your mates, in both kinds of club. And that's about Class, I suppose. Or is it just about mates? It reflected the schools in the Town, one a Grammar , one a Sec. Mod., and one a Catholic Sec. Mod., and the clubs reflected the schools' populations

The adults in the Church Club thanked me nervously, and asked if I had enjoyed myself. I said I had, very much, and would come again, if they would have me. I asked if all the girls went to church, as it was called the Church Club. They laughed. "No, none of them do. Oh, maybe one or two at Christmastime. No, they say they've grow too old now to bother about going to church. They're polite about it, they say they're not atheists, but they say they've outgrown religion." They looked a bit sad as they told me this, as they obviously hoped their offspring would get the same thing out of churchgoing as they did, but it plainly was not going to happen.

I went back a few times, but I began to feel they tolerated me, and didn't need me. They could have managed fine without their mothers too, but were well-bred enough not to say so.

STEP NINE --- WINDING UP AND WINDING DOWN

"In every act consider what precedes and what follows, and then proceed to the act. If you do not consider, you will at first begin with spirit, since you have not thought at all of the things which will follow; but afterwards, when some consequences have shown themselves, you will basely desist."

The Roman Stoic, Epictetus, The Discourses, Book Three .

I was educated to be a rubber technologist, and that is what my degree is in. This has caused much ribald merriment amongst my friends, who refer to 'rubber goods' and such. Without rubber they would have to ride their cars and bikes on rails, aircraft could not land safely, pipes could not seal easily, papers would fly all over without rubber bands. It is a much-despised material which carries out its humble task without complaint, is taken for granted: yet the failure of one seal on that disastrous rocket explosion killed seven astronauts. I got interested in it when doing chemistry at school, as it was clearly a chemical, yet I was not told what kind of chemical. I now know it is a polymer, a long chain of simple units, sometimes hundreds of thousands long. Mostly the units are made of carbon and hydrogen, although chlorine and nitrogen, even silicon, fit in to some synthetic polymers, for specialist uses.

The first rubber used was natural rubber, from a tree in the Brazilian rain-forest. Seeds were stolen in the late Nineteenth Century by a caddish Englishman, and taken, via Kew Gardens, to Malaya. In WW2 the Japanese invaded Malaya, so our rubber supplies for war vehicles were cut off. The Americans had foreseen this, and made synthetic rubber out of alcohol, generated by fermenting surplus wheat. They made others, like neoprene, which resisted oil, and was discovered by an Englishman, Carothers, who also invented Nylon before committing suicide.

All rubbers are made of these long strings that behave like a spring, which is why even raw rubber is bouncy. But when it gets hot, it softens and droops, getting sticky and rather messy. It was used to make Macintoshes, named after the inventor, a Scotsman, but in hot weather they stuck to your clothes and picked up bits of fluff, and were generally useless. An American, Charles Goodyear, was messing around with raw rubber, and mixed some with sulphur. He left it on a stove and fell asleep. On waking, he found that instead of being a sticky mess, it was tough yet still rubbery. He had 'cured' it, and soon manufacturers were mixing all sorts of chemicals in to speed up this process, which became know as 'Vulcanisation', after Vulcan, the Roman God of Fire.

It was later discovered what the chemistry of vulcanisation was. The long polymer chains were connected together by sulphur so that they did not slip past each other when they wriggled faster on getting hotter. The sulphur was a 'cross-link', and was essential to useful rubber. If you made too many cross-links, the rubber became hard and inflexible, and was called ebonite. It went to make pipe-stems, but little else.

At the age I had now reached, I began to see myself as Vulcan, the cross-linker, joining huge organisations together that might otherwise slip around when the going got hot, and melt. I was not a joiner of the main chain, that was not so useful, as they had many units already. I was the little bunch of atoms that linked two chains together to form a much more useful whole, one that could stand moderate heat, and could not be dissolved in any solvent. If I disappeared, then the chains would revert to what they were before, but not as useful.

An American President, I think Johnson, said he would rather have a rebel inside his tent pissing out than outside the tent pissing in. He implied that pissing was what the rebel had to do, there was no choice; presumably all the Good People, the joiners, his friends, didn't piss at all. I stood outside everyone's tent, not pissing anywhere, but trying to explain one tent to another, so we could all fight better. I probably pissed on my own boots, but that is another matter.

The Elcaster Youth Project used up all its funds when Stanley took his money elsewhere, as he had to, because the Charity Commission would not let him fund the same project for long. Without funds, we could not employ a co-ordinator, so Rob left. So did I. I never liked having to beg for money, fill in all those lengthy forms asking 'how does your scheme benefit crippled black lesbian dwarfs?' Some remained, councillors and committee experts, to raise money to fulfil the aims of our constitution. The first thing they did was to abolish the condition that you couldn't come in as a representative, and sure enough, the Youth Service, and others, joined up to tick their little boxes. It made no difference. they were impotent, and did nothing.

The County had a bit of a conscience about Elcaster

having no youth club, so they sent two Street Workers along. Neither had much experience, and only about three weeks' training, but they were eager, and female, and paid regularly. The EYP were supposed to direct them, but as none of the committee had any experience of youth work at all, so they used to come to me and talk over what they were doing. I had no position at all, merely experience, and I certainly didn't want to rejoin my baby, the EYP, as it was now just a hot air machine for blowing useless bubbles.

The two street workers were really good, full of enthusiasm. They went out on the streets of Elcaster for two hours a week, found youths where they congregated, and just talked to them. They could put them in touch with youth organisations if they wanted it, but mostly they didn't. The kids just wanted what they always want, an adult to listen to them. And Maree and Jenny listened. They heard the stories that kids tell credulous adults, but Maree was streetwise, coming as she did from Glasgow. She knew enough not to put them down, though. They were both genuinely interested in young people on the streets, for whatever reason.

Maree wanted to turn the back room of her off-licence on the High Street into a small youth club. I encouraged her, as she knew what she was doing and had a real rapport with the kids, who respected her. But the usual thing happened when she told her neighbours. They protested in the strongest ways possible, writing to the council, objecting to the suitability of the room. They threw the book at poor

Maree. The kids would go into her shop and talk to her at all times when she was open. Maree's husband was very tolerant, and allowed it.

Customers were not always so forgiving, though. Some objected to pushing past teenagers to get their booze, and sometimes complained to the police, although Maree was very careful not to sell them anything illegal, despite their frequent requests.

The EYP paid for her to go on a short Counselling course, run by the Workers Ed. in Studley. I decided to go with her, as I was interested in seeing if I wanted to be a counsellor as well. It was only six weeks long, and I thought it might be fun.

It was fun, and fascinating too. The lecturer was well experienced, and an amusing talker. There was one other man besides me, and four women. The first week we practised just listening to each other in pairs, and not showing boredom. I was with one of the other women, and I talked to Maree on the way home about what we had done.

"Did you enjoy that, Maree? I certainly did."

"Aye, but we'll have to see Annie about that other bloke."

"You mean the lecturer?" Of course, women always know each other's first names, after about ten seconds.

"Aye, but that bloke's not right. Not right at all." She wouldn't tell me what was not right about him, but he didn't turn up at the next session. I assume the women had had a word with Annie, and told her what he had said to the one he was working with. Something inappropriate to women, because they all thought the same. I became worried about myself.

They all laughed. "You just aren't the same at all, Bill. You're a pussycat!", and they laughed again. I was glad not to be thrown out, but what did they mean by 'pussycat'? I still don't know.

We continued to learn how to do counselling, how to look as if you're listening, not to look at the clock whilst you do so, how to ask non-judgmental questions, how to seem empathic (that word is used a lot, 'empathy'. I still don't know exactly what it means, but then I don't think many counsellors do either.). We worked mainly in pairs, with a different partner each week. It dawned on me that all the others, including Maree, were there not to become counsellors, but to find out if counselling would do them good. It was a very relaxed atmosphere, thank to our lecturer, who was a specialist in grief counselling, and I made up my mind early on that if I ever need that, she would do the job superbly.

On about the fourth session, we all sat around and told all the others of the worst times in our lives. You would have thought it would be gloom-laden and serious, but it was quite the opposite. We all laughed out loud at the weird things that had happened to each of us, the odd ways of thinking we had had, and how we had eventually got our heads straight and began to think logically about what had occurred. It was so funny that our sides ached afterwards. It was a superb way to show us how useful counselling can be, if it helps us to get our heads round the situation and begin to think reasonably.

I was commended for my 'empathic nodding' when listening to others, and everyone got praise of some sort from the lecturer, and no criticism of any kind. As a man, I wondered if this was sensible, as we could not be much good yet, and I wanted to know what I had to develop if I were to go on a full course. Maree said this was typical of a man, and that women didn't work like that. Maybe that is why most counsellors are women. Men just suffer in silence and can take their worries to the grave, unrevealed.

On the last night, we begged our lecturer to continue the course, as we were all enjoying it so much. She said she wouldn't get paid by the WEA, as six weeks was the maximum, and if we wanted, we could enrol on a full course somewhere else. She emphasised that we were never to be judgmental, never offer solutions, we had to get clients to come to their own solutions. I realised that I would therefore never make a counsellor, as I always would make a few suggestions as to what clients should do to get over their problems. I was a teacher, after all, it was engraved on my very soul to tell people what to do, even if they ignored you, which they ought. We went on for an extra hour that last night, but it had to end eventually, and many of us were in tears as we said good-bye, including our tutor. It had been a great experience. I did go some years later to courses at Oxford University on Cognitive Behaviour Therapy, with a view to improving my dealings with the mentally troubled people I was meeting at a Day Centre in Stratford, but it was never as much fun as those six weeks had been.

Maree was irrepressible. Having had her youth club behind the shop idea knocked on the head by nasty neighbours, she found a man who worked for the Youth Service in Stratford. He encouraged her to do something different, he could see she had talent at working with teenagers. She was determined to find a place to run a youth club, or a 'shelter', as she put it, somewhere to get out of the rain and cold in the winter, if nothing else. She wanted to ask the Grogg Hall, and I simply shrugged my shoulders and wished her luck. I had had enough of their snobbery and rejection, but I underestimated the power of a charming woman.

She persuaded the Chairman to let her have a hut, which was not being used for anything except storage, and was right outside the caretaker's house, well away from the main buildings. It didn't look much, she told me, but we could do it up, paint it how the kids want it, Bill, it's perfect. I was uneasy about her doing it on her own, as Jenny had started her own family by now, and Maree was on her own. I knew what could happen to solo women in an Elcaster youth club, so I said I would come with her.

The man from Stratford, Bob, came too, when he could. He was also a Glaswegian, and when those two got excited and chattered away, I could hardly understand a word they said. But it went brilliantly right from the start. Maree had made good relationships with a lot of youngsters, and they all came to the Hut, as it became know. They were normal teenagers, and there were some Grammar-school kids amongst them, which was unusual, but I was glad to see them. Soon we had over twenty a night; we cadged paint and brushes from B&Q in Stratford, and decorated the whole place. The Greig trustees gave permission,as it was no skin off their nose, it improved the place. There were two rooms, and the kids divided it into a Girl's half and a Boy's half. The Girl's half was painted in deep pastel colours, with stars on the ceiling, the Boy's half in panels of primary colours, and white where they couldn't decide. It looked really good when they had finished. The spirited worker from Connexions, who came to help most nights, spilled a can of paint on the carpet, and we couldn't stop laughing. That paint patch is till there, even though the hut is just a storeroom again now, pushed aside when they built the extension to the Sports Hall, and unable to be used as a youth club any more, alas.

The club ran like clockwork for many weeks. We only had the older age-group, who had been friends with Maree when she was working on the streets, and they kept the younger kids away. This always happens, the older ones do not have the same tastes as the youngsters, and they want their club the way they want it, not full of annoying tiddlers. But I knew that unless we attracted younger ones, the club could fold when the older ones were of an age where they were accepted into pubs, and a youth club was something they had left behind, as is natural. We had a new worker, Kath, who was very quiet and cast down at first. I suspected she had had a hard time, and was getting over it, even though she was not yet thirty. She was working behind the till in a supermarket, a job well below her capabilities, as she was clearly intelligent and capable. Slowly we gave her more and more to do, and she grew in confidence before our eyes. She had the right attitude, tolerant of much of their behaviour; she could swear with the best of them, but she spoke up when they were really rude, and she knew how to talk to them. They respected Kath from the start, and she clearly liked the work.

We had a few hiccups, as all youth clubs do, a few complaints from other users when they went round to the back to annoy the other groups, as kids will. We always tried to sort it out on the spot. Darren, the Greig Sports Hall worker was always getting the rough end of the stick from them, because he would always react to their teasing. He was not much older than they were, and they used to delight in winding him up. We tried to calm him down, and even told him that they were doing it on purpose because they loved to watch his temper flare, but it took a long time for him to understand what we were saying. He did eventually, and would often take them out on the tennis court for football, or basketball, which was good of him, as it was not what he was being paid for by the Grogg.

One night, a lad I had known in the previous club, Andrew, came down, and greeted me effusively. I knew him of old, he could be trouble if he was in the wrong mood, and so it proved. He had offered me a roll-up when he was only nine years old, one day when we were burning the old sofas at the Trades hut, before we gave it to the footballers. He thought of himself as a 'hard nut', and his father certainly was, but we had always got along fine, his father and me. He told me what a pain his son could be, and we laughed about it.

Andrew decided to see if I had changed, as we used to clash in the old days over his behaviour, and he had been temporarily excluded a few times. So he decided to lean on the door when Maree and I were outside smoking. We could not get in; this was typical of his previous way of winding me up, when he was twelve. I sighed, and decided I had to do something, otherwise who knew how far he might go. He was starting to kick at the soft board walls, and I had to act now. So I pushed the door open, went in, and grabbed his collar to throw him out, knowing that talking to him was worse than useless. He swore me up in heaps, but never showed any aggression as I propelled him towards the door. I had known him since he was nine, and he was not going to hit me now. I gave him a shove and he went down the steps, still swearing and vowing all sorts of ill upon my head. I just stood and laughed at him. "Don't hurry back, Andrew, if that's how you're going to behave. Aren't you a bit too old for this kind of thing now? This club is not for lads of your age, you're old enough to go down to the pub." I knew he had been banned from all the Elcaster pubs, but he got my drift, and went off muttering.

Maree had bolted by this time, not knowing what to do. All the kids in the club were scared, so they went home, and I found myself alone in the club. So I told the Greig staff that the club was closing early, and went home.

Later that week, I had a visit from Bob, the County youth worker. We sat down, and I knew what he had come about.

"Bill, you can't do that sort of thing now. You cannot lay a finger on them."

"No, Bob, YOU can't lay a finger on them, it's in your work conditions. But I am a volunteer. I was stopping any further damage to the Grogg's building."

"Aye, I know that. But you might have been assaulted. Or he might take you to court for assault."

"Oh come on, Bob. With all those witnesses, and his reputation? I'm an Elcaster person, I know who he is, and how he behaves. I was acting to defend my property."

"No, seriously, Bill. the County rules say you must not assault them, no matter what they do."

"Well, I am entitled to act in self-defence. What would you have done in that situation, then, Bob?"

"I would have had to let him continue and send for the police."

"And turn the whole thing into a possible prosecution? He's in enough trouble for other things as it is. I did what was necessary, and it's over now. Finished. He won't come back, he found out I hadn't changed, and he's satisfied."

"Well, I'll have to report the incident, Bill, to my superiors."

"Fine. I don't work for them, and you do. If you are saying that as a volunteer I have to obey every petty rule of the County, then you'll have to tell me not to come back, and I'll start another club of my own. But let's not get wound up about it. It hasn't happened to me for years, and it won't happen again. OK?"

"OK, Bill. Let's just forget it."

But Andrew did come back, two weeks later. My heart sank when I saw him sauntering up, but I could not show that, so I said, "Hi, Andrew."

"Hi, Bill. Want a roll-up?" He had rolled up several fags, one of which he gave to me with a flourish. We chatted, not about the recent incident, but about old times, and how things had changed.

"Not everything's changed, Andrew. I haven't changed."

"No, you haven't, have you, you old sod. You're just the same awkward bugger that you were."

"And so are you, Andrew, so are you. How's your Dad?"
I never saw him again at the club. His public image was intact, he had faced me out, and so was mine. He went to jail later. He was not one we had rescued, but he was still a part of Elcaster, still a citizen of our Town, and he was owed some respect.

Andrew was not the only Old Boy of the youth club that I kept in touch with. I was beginning to see youngsters come to the club whose parents had been members of my first club. I would get a huge buzz out of saying, "You think you're a lot of trouble, don't you? Well, I remember your mother, and believe me, you are not half a s wicked as she was." One boy in particular had organised a Roller blade Skateathon to raise money to repair the decaying wooden skate park. He had done a terrific job, about twenty of them roller bladed round and round the Sports Hall for hours, and they raised over £200. But Darren would not get round to collecting the money off his mates. It was hard for him, I knew, but he had organised it, and they were letting him down. So one night I said to him, "If you don't get on with it right this minute, I am coming round to see your Mum about it."

He took a huff and said he was going home, so I followed him, as I did not know exactly where he lived. On the way I saw his brother, also an old club member, and asked if his Mum was at home. He said she was, so I went up to the door that Darren had disappeared through, and knocked. I saw Darren watching through the window, expecting to see his Mum give me short shrift and send me home.

To his surprise, his Mum came to the door, and greeted me with a big hug. "Bill, lovely to see you. What's the trouble?" It was Big Mol, one of my favourite trouble making girls from my first club. She was often very naughty, but always with a twinkle in her eye, never malicious.

I told her the trouble, and young Darren sidled into the room, eyes downcast. He thought he was in for a telling off. I said, "Don't be cross with him, Mol, he has done really well, only he's having trouble collecting the cash off his mates. Let's help him, eh?" So we sat down and Mol put a scheme together that would persuade the kids to pay up. Mostly it involved Mol threatening to have a word with their parents, and this worked, because Mol was a seriously scary woman when roused, and everyone on the Estate knew it. She hadn't changed.

Some of the encounters did not have a happy ending. One lad had died of an overdose of heroin at 29, a pleasant lad. He had sworn at me one night, so I swore back, and he returned the curse. "Oh, let's have a swearing match." I said. "My turn now. I bet I know a lot more swearwords than you do, because I'm older."

"I'm going to get my Dad," he said, and walked out of

the club. I followed him, saying, "Oh, great. let's involve your Dad too, let's make a real match of it!" I left him a little way up the road. There is a limit to how much humiliation a kid should take.

I have known three or four youth club kids who died of their drug habits, and it always makes me sad, especially if I have to go to their funerals. It makes no difference to tell modern kids that I have known a young man, standing where they are now, say "I can control my drug-taking," only to have them die years later because they couldn't. It's not all that high a percentage, though, especially as nowadays all of them try weed at some time or another. Few go on to the harder drugs, I think, because they know the difference in effect between weed and the hard stuff, and are aware of the dangers.

One boy committed suicide, for unknown reasons, and I was asked to talk about him at the funeral by his brother, both of whom I had known at the youth club. That was hard, as he was not very old, and I had not seen him for several years. The only consolation is that I get to see many old members, who are always polite and able to tell me what they have been doing since I saw them last. I guess that the ones who have not been successful don't go to their comrade's funerals.

AFTER THE SUICIDE OF S*****N A****D, FUNERAL

1ST OCTOBER 1999

Why did you rush off? Why could you not wait a bit,
The trees were on the turn, they looked so lovely in the sun,
And leaves were raining down like tears.
Where was the hurry? You could have rested up;
Instead, you took a one-way ticket, not to Blackpool,
As you told your friends, but out. Right out.
A bit impulsive, drastic, even. Now you're gone,
A lot of people wish they'd done much more,
But still can't think of what, exactly. Nor could you.
The turbulent, slow-moving river of your family moves on
Timelessly. They cannot help you now.
You've sunk beneath the surface, out of sight,
But I still see you, smiling your tight defensive smile
Under the brown autumn water.

As younger members joined us, Maree confessed that she couldn't get on with them as well as she had the ones she had met on the streets. Perhaps there was something about meeting them in all weathers, sharing a smoke, which she was not allowed to do in the Hut. There were more rules in an enclosed space, and more youngsters around too. She left to go nursing in Cornwall. I would bet she takes up youth work again some time, even though she had little kids of her own. Once you are bitten with the youth club bug, really bitten as I had been, it never leaves your blood. It's like a drug, you have to get your fix, and you don't know why, because it's hard and unpleasant at first. You feel old and a failure, but you carry on because you know you have something driving you that you are not able to resist. You know it will be all right some time, as it always is, but it never gets to be relaxing, never gets to be a good feeling all the time, some times not for weeks, but eventually, in the dark hours of the night, you know why you do it, you know why you carry on despite all the difficulties. It's because it's in your soul. You reflect on all the tiny things that happened, that were said by the kids to you, and you know why you do it. Your soul requires it. You cannot explain this to anyone, sometimes even to yourself, but every youth worker who loves their job will tell you the same. It's not about doing them good, keeping them off the streets, helping them, guiding them to a better life. It may or may not be any or all of those, but deep down it is about human contact, real solid contact that you can almost touch, see, smell, feel. It's not even the feeling you get as a teacher, because your pupils have to be in school, by Law, and they do not choose to be there. Maybe most would, but the ones you meet in a youth club mostly would not be in school if it were voluntary. So if they go to the club, it's because they want to. If they talk to you, it's because they want to. If they ask you things, its because they want to know what you think, how you will react. And if they don't like what you give them, they will say so, and not talk to you again. They are as shy as wild animals, and if they come to you, you feel privileged. As when a wild bird chooses to settle on your outstretched finger and your heart skips a beat with joy for a second, so it sometimes is with kids at a youth club.

Sometimes, though, it's just plain boring, and both of you are just passing the time.

In fact, it's mostly like that. But the romantic bit is what keeps you coming back.

The Elcaster Youth Project stuttered back into half-life as the Town Council wanted to provide a Youth Shelter near the local shopping precinct. Tesco's were complaining that Wicked Youths were terrorising shoppers, and the police were helpless, as they always are. So it was thought that a Shelter near the precinct would attract the aforesaid Youths and make them less terrifying to the adults. This was a real problem, and difficult to deal with, and confrontation by adults or police always makes it worse. At least the Shelter might provide a long-term partial solution. The Town Council wanted the EYP to act as banker, to take the money from the grant giver authorities, and pay it into our bank account, and later give it to the Shelter providers. This seemed innocuous, so the Treasurer and I agreed. We were now the only remaining members of the EYP Committee, and we did not want lots of work, since we had done our share, thank you.

Tesco's were miserably mean over the whole thing, and made it plain that they were a business, not a charity. The argument that by providing a Shelter we would improve their business and increase their profit met with a total denial. I shall never shop at Tesco's again, apart from the odd ice-cream. And their chocolate cake. And... All right, I shan't shop there much.

THE CASE OF THE YOUTH NON-SHELTER

Once upon a time, almost two years ago, in a Town called Elcaster, some good people had an idea that would benefit many in that Town. They would build a shelter that youngsters would go into when they wanted somewhere private that was not home, nor the streets, nor anywhere that they might be a nuisance. For they were a nuisance at times, they collected around Tesco's and intimidated the shoppers, and hung around Moorfields and made loud noises, and sat on the Old Persons bench outside the Church. They used the Tesco's doorway because it was central, and it had some shelter from the rain. The police had to be called, and they issued AntiSocial Behaviour Orders,ASBOs, to the kids, and made it a restricted area, which annoyed the kids, so there was friction between the police and the youngsters, who ignored the ASBOs.

The youngsters made a good point to the Town. They had nowhere to go, the only Youth Club was open for a mere 2 hours a week. Nothing had been provided for them since the Skate park was knocked down after only 9 years of life, due to it being wooden and built on soil, and therefore having gone rotten.

The police had a good idea. They suggested a Youth

Shelter, made of steel and tough clear plastic, with some sports facilities round it, to be put up behind Tesco's. The kids thought this was a good idea, so did the Town Councillors consulted, so did the Youth Club workers, so did everybody, in fact. Tesco's refused to give any money towards it, which was mean, but, hey, they only made £3 Billion profit that year. So the County found £15K, and the youth workers got the kids to select the shelter they wanted (one like the Studley shelter), and the site was chosen with care by the police, because if it were in the wrong place it would not attract youngsters, and so would not reduce the crime of breaking ASBOs. Everybody agreed, this was the shelter, this was the place.

Then the trouble started. The good folk were told that no planning permission was needed. Then they were told that it WAS needed, so the forms were filled in, with great difficulty as is usual. Then the Stratford District Council could not agree with Elcaster Town Council about who owned the land. I thought the People of Elcaster owned the public land, but I was wrong. These things caused a delay of over a year! The kids got cynical. Broken promises, as usual, just as Bill Bayley had told Mrs. Juned, and made her cry. (The kids clapped him for it. Now who was right? He was ashamed, though).

So there was yet another meeting with the police, Town Councillors, youth workers, and a County Councillor. What was the delay, exactly? It seemed that lighting was needed, so the police bravely volunteered to provide the cost of £7K. Great! The Town Councillors asked about the cost of maintenance. Very low, said the police expert, almost none for seven years. So hooray, all we needed was the Town Council Subcommittee to approve it, and as the Town Council had been consulted all along, no problems were anticipated. Except from Councillor Barking, who didn't like the shelter and proposed another, for ages 6-14, and he didn't like the site, and suggested that kids playground by Oversley House. He said something about future development behind Tesco's, but gave no information.

So you can guess what happened. Mr. Barking's little Subcommittee turned it down. They want it in Another Place (not Hell, presumably). So it's back to Planning Permission all over again. Talk about Deja Vu! Will there be lighting? Hopefully. There will certainly be CCTV, which exists already. Will the kids go in it? We do not know, since they approved the original place, and may not like their wishes denied. Watch this space. You will find me in the shelter, if it's ever built.

It was built, not in the place intended, but in the old kids playground. It kind of worked too, because intimidation at the precinct has reduced, and the kids do play in it, and climb on the top of it. Therein lies another problem. An old lady in the Old People's Home on the other side of the road says that kids can look right into her bathroom now, and she objects to it. The kids fall about laughing when questioned on the subject, then deny it utterly. What us? Look at an old lady in the bath? D'you think we're psychos? Urrrgggh! And they fall about laughing again, which means that they certainly do what the old dear says. But what can anyone do about it? Get some frosted glass, dear, and remember you were young once. Or perhaps not.

The Hut was going well, and I was also the Editor of a monthly magazine of Writers, the Bear Flag. It had grown out of the EYP writing group for youngsters, as the old continued it. We had been running for about a year, when we put on the Teddy Awards Evening, in the Town Hall. People were given Teddies for outstanding performance, and we gave cash prizes to kids for writing something for the Bear Flag. It was a great evening, but no-one from the youth club took part. I tried to get some of them to write something, but it was like getting blood out of a stone. "Writing's boring, it's what we do at school." was the reply. I got one girl to agree, but when she never gave me anything, I sat down and talked to her, then wrote down what she had said. I kept it anonymous, in case she got trouble from her school. It was a 'wow' in the Bear Flag. Loads of people complained about the language, and how easy kids have it now, not like when I was a girl, and so on and on. I pointed out to the female critics that all they had had to do then was find a husband, and keep him, then have a family. His wages paid the rent. Now, men are less dependable, wages are relatively lower, you need two wage-packets to run a family, a girl cannot depend on keeping either a man or a job, change is faster, social pressure is greater, sex may be safer but it's compulsory, and so on and on. They saw what I meant, I think, or maybe they retained their prejudices intact.

A GIRL'S LIFE IN ELCASTER

My life in Elcaster is shit. I'm a girl, I'm in my last year at school, and I can't wait to get out. Get out of Elcaster, I mean. This place has nothing for me, even though I've lived here all my life. Some life! What is there to do here? Get out of school, get off your face on weed and alcohol down in the field. That's in the summer, in the winter you can't even do that. Most of my mates do it, it's not just me. You can get a bit of a laugh sometimes at school, but mostly it's boredom, wall-to-wall. There's one teacher there, I swear I'm going to die before she does, so that I can come back and haunt her to death. I really hate her, and she hates me, I think. She must do, the way she goes on at me all the time.

I don't go to church, not at all, not ever. I don't believe in God, how can there be a God and let all this shit happen? He must be some kind of sadist to do that. Free will? What's free about it? Nothing's free in this life, except being bored. I don't know what happens to you after you're dead. Nothing, I imagine. Just a big black Nothing. Like Elcaster on a wet Monday morning, when you've got Science first thing, and you haven't done your course work.

The men are all right, in a way. Well, they're not men, are they, just boys really. They put themselves around, they're players, which the girls aren't, or else we're called slags. They think they're cool and tough, but they're not,

not really. They are fit! You can have a laugh with some of them, at times. Others are just boring, or annoying. They think they're so fascinating and grown up, but they act like silly little kids. Why don't they grow up?

I'm not going to have any kids, I think. Well, I don't know, at the moment I think I won't, but you never know. I'm certainly not getting married! Look at all my friends' parents, hardly any of them still together. I'd make marriage illegal, put people in prison for doing it. It really screws you up, does marriage.

I want to be famous, and come back to Elcaster and tell them what a pokey little place this is. I don't know what I will be famous at. I can't sing, anyway I'm too old to be a Pop Star. Maybe an actress, or something like that. Anything that gets you lots of money, because money is the way to a Good Life, and you can't deny it. I want to be rich. I may marry a rich guy, as long as he dies soon after. Yeah, I know I said marriage was bad, but this would have a purpose to it, like.

My Mum knows all this. She knows. I don't suppose she likes it much, but she sees why I think like this. She probably thought the same when she was my age. Although she wouldn't have done the grass, it wasn't around then. I don't do pills or anything else, scag is really out. It's just weed and alcohol for me. It keeps me kind of fit, in a way.

Some things are really phat, like having a laugh with your mates at school, when you're in a lesson where you can muck about. I don't hate all the teachers, some of them are OK, well, some of the time. I'm going to do Business Studies when I leave, if I can get the right place to do it. I'll have to go to college, but I think that might be phat too. You don't do much work, it's not like GCSEs, and they're lecturers there, they treat you a bit more like an adult.

My future? I've got no future, not here in this place. I suppose I'll get a job. I've had one here for ages, part-time, and it's shit. I know I'll have to earn my own living one day, and work for it. I just want to have a good time, a laugh. Like I said, my life in Elcaster is shit.

Eight years later, I did the same with one of the boys that came to my house, to the One Henley Street Club, since by this time, 2010, there was no youth club running.

A YOUNG MAN'S LIFE IN ALCESTER

I'm not giving my name. That's why I wear a hood most of the time, so no-one knows who I am. Like that girl said in your paper years ago, my life in Alcester is shit. I've left school, thank goodness. They never liked me there, I was just a nuisance to them. I know I played around a bit with my mates, but it was the teachers job to keep us in order, wasn't it? I wasn't much good at anything really, except IT.., which meant I could get onto the Internet. Anyway, they chucked me out before I took any exams. I went to the PRU (Pupil Referral Unit) for a bit, but I didn't go very often, and they wouldn't let me take any GCSEs from there. So I've got no passes. Nothing to show for eleven years in education. Yes, I can read and write OK, but I don't like doing either.

I don't do much in the daytime, except hang out with my mates, or sleep. Most of them are like me, no exams, hated school. My Dad gets fed up with me, when he's at home. He's away a lot, he's a lorry driver and he works all hours, sometimes he's away for days at a time. He says I should get a job, but he doesn't understand, there aren't any around. He says he's been working ever since he left school. He didn't get any exams either, but he started working on the land, weeding and such. Those jobs aren't around any more. He learned to drive when he was 17, he saved the money to pay for his test, but now it costs £200 or more to take a driving test. He just doesn't understand, he goes down to the pub and leaves Mum to 'deal' with me.

Mum's OK, she gives me money and tells me not to tell my Dad. I smoke fags when I can afford them, and sometimes Mum gives me the money to buy them. She says I have to have some fun in life. She gets on at me about doing nothing, and tries to get me up in the morning, but what's the point? I sleep late because me and my mates go out at night until late. Nobody bothers you late at night, you can do what you want without nosy parkers watching you like you were a criminal all the time.

Yes, I have been in trouble with the coppers. We like to climb on the roofs of empty buildings at night, and we got reported and caught. We weren't actually doing anything, but they said we were trespassing, and gave us an official caution. We have done a bit of vandalism around the Town, mostly because we dare each other to do things. We like to take risks, it makes us feel good. Especially when we get away with it.

Mostly it's very boring in Alcester. There isn't even a Youth Club now, hasn't been one for two years. We're too young to go to the pubs, they know our ages and throw us out. We sometimes get drink, like beer and vodka, if one of us has an older brother or cousin, and some of the Mums give us drink occasionally. But usually they haven't got the money.

We all smoke weed. It takes away that bored feeling for a time, it's better than drink for that. It's not that expensive, but it can be hard to get. If we get a stash and sell some to our mates, the cops say that's dealing, and you can go to prison for it. Skunk weed sends you mad, they say, but sometimes I'd rather be mad than bored out of my skull here in Alcester. Nobody cares whether we live or die, except our Mums, we're just a nuisance to most people. Well, if we're going to be a nuisance, lets do the job properly, I say. Maybe I'll start on the hard drugs, there's money to be made dealing in that. Can't see where else I can get money, except the occasional job on the fair at weekends. I don't like to think about the future.

We had five good years in the Hut, proper youth work, no damage to the building, few expenses, since we had no room to play games like Table Football, Pool or Table

Tennis. The kids came and sat on the steps at the front in the Summer, and we got fewer of them in the Winter when going outside was cold. Smoking was banned inside, but we could never do anything about it when they puffed away outside, except try to talk to them about the risks, and get experts in to test their Carbon Monoxide levels, as a bit of fun with a serious purpose. I was delighted to find my own CO level was as low as a non-smoker, since as a pipe-smoker I do not inhale. I tried to get kids interested in smoking a pipe, instead of fags, if they felt they had to smoke at all, but it was always a failure. They think I smoke wacky baccy in it anyway, but many youngsters have had a puff on my pipe, just to see what it's like, to the horror of professional youth workers.

The County Service were becoming more and more intrusive with their activities. They brought out a kind of 'syllabus', with headings such as 'Health', 'Civics', 'Religion', which we were supposed to get the kids to participate in, and there were boxes to be ticked, and if they weren't ticked, then you had to get on and do it somehow. I thought it was becoming more and more like school, and said so. I was ignored, since these edicts were coming from On High, probably government level, to judge by the scale of the silliness.

One night the kids themselves rebelled. As Kate, who was now the senior youth worker, tried to get them engaged in some worthy activity from the syllabus book, they resisted and she told them 'they had to, because it was down here in the book.' This set Darryl off.

"This youth club is become like f***ing school, ent it!"

"Be quiet, Darryl, let's just get on with it."

"No, I bloody ent! Nor are any of us! That's right, ent it , lads?"

"Darryl, don't be silly. Let's start then. Who knows about healthy eating?"

"Sod healthy eating! We're going on strike, right lads?"

"You can't go on strike, Darryl, you aren't working." Kate was always cool and logical. Darryl had his dander up, though.

"Come on lads, this is a sit-down strike!" And they all sat down around the room, and folded their arms implacably.

"Right, then. If you don't want to do as I ask, you can all go home."

"NO, we f***ing won't go anywhere, we're on strike." They all nodded.

Kate was taken aback. She hadn't met passive resistance before, and was at a loss to know what to do. She nodded her head towards the Girl's Room, where I joined her.

"What can we do, Bill? They won't go home."

"Well, I did say that your syllabus was too much like school, and I sympathise with them, a bit."

"Did you put them up to it? I wouldn't be surprised if...."

"No, Kate, I wouldn't do that to you. What do we do? We do nothing."

"What, we stay in here?"

"No, we join them, sit beside them, get them talking, ask them about their feelings, ask them what they want to do, we can tick all those boxes of yours, even the healthy eating if we ask them why they don't want to talk about it."

So that's what we did. they were all very vocal, letting their resentments out in colourful phrases, and they went home cheerfully at nine, having had a great night, and having made their point.

Kate and I went through the syllabus, and it was amazing how many boxes we could tick just from the half-hour of chat we had had with them.

"Ticking boxes is simple, Kate. If one of them swears, says 'Jesus!', tick the box for having discussed Religion. Just let's do what we always do, then have ten minutes at the end of the evening, when they've all gone home, and tick the boxes then. The arses who wrote that stuff can never check up on you, can they? If necessary, a wholehearted lie is always best, rather than ruin the evening by doing things they hate. They're right. This is not school, they get enough of that in the day. Just because the government pay your salary doesn't mean they can dictate what we do. They don't own our souls."

Kate was a bright girl, and she saw my point at once. From then on we had a laugh fitting what had gone on in the club to the didactic rubbish that was in the syllabus.

There were problems, of course, there always are in youth clubs. One regular one was Ryan. Ryan was 'a sandwich short of a picnic', to coin a phrase, but the kids mostly tolerated him, as he was easily amused. The trouble was that he wanted to control the music player. The other kids didn't always like his choice of tapes, and tried to take the player from him. This ended in a row, always. The adults took it in turns to sort it out. At first, Ryan would leave in a huff, which was not ideal, but it was sorted. Later, he got to stand up for himself more, and he was a growing lad, getting stronger. Father came down to help sometimes, but he didn't improve matters. We just had to sort out a compromise night after night. Sometimes you just get to act as a policeman.

We had some excellent youth workers, from other areas. One, Hank, came from the North of the County, and it was a rest home for him. Our kids think they are tough, but compared with really rough areas they are pussycats. Hank gave us lots of ideas, and he was a nice man as well. We had some volunteers too, who wanted to train so they could get paid. One man came from Long Lartin, the maximum security prison nearby. He tried so hard, poor man, but eventually he had to leave. The contrast between how the prisoners had to treat him, and how our kids treated him, was just too great. We always used to have a drink after youth club in the Grogg bar, to discuss what had gone on during the evening, who was going out with who, and those times were some of the best I ever had in youth work. We all had the right attitude towards the kids, not laughing at them or despising them, but taking them for what they were, young human beings. We were only responsible for their safety, but we cared about them as people too, but there was a limit to what we could, or should, do. We hoped they would not get into trouble outside, and we would support them if they did, but we were not a school, proud of our reputation. What reputation does a youth club have anyway, in the public eye? But we were very proud of our kids all right, there was no mistake about that.

It came to an end, as all good things do, when the Grogg were extending their Sports Hall, and the Hut was in the way. So one Summer it was the last night there in the Hut, and the kids wrote messages on the walls, some crude, but some fond. It had been almost the perfect site for a youth club, away from adults but near enough to be noticed, near enough to the caretakers house to prevent vandalism, yet we had it all to ourselves. I thought, never mind, another place will soon come along. Let's just wait and see.

STEP TEN -- PREPARING FOR THE END

We were given space at the Grogg Centre in the Green Room, the room behind the stage. It was all they could offer us, they said. The previous Grogg Chair had left, and the new one at least had some conscience that the Grogg should try to accommodate a youth club. The room was quite unsuitable, being too small and we had to share it with whoever used the stage for productions. We had to clear away everything each night, always a chore. Kate kept on as senior youth worker, but we lost all the older members, who thought nothing of the cramped conditions. The younger ones who came were unruly, and we had to do a lot of policing, as the huts around were where the adult groups met, and our kids loved to cause a nuisance, if they were allowed to. We had a hard job keeping them amused, without any games or space to do much in the way of activities. It was about half the size of our Hut, which was itself too small to fit games in. I tried telling ghost stories, which was popular, we painted T-shirts, played chess and cards, but it was an inadequate area to be a proper youth club.

One winter's night, in a bitter frost, we arrived to find the door locked. Darren, one of the Sports hall workers, told us that Basil Buckingham, who was in charge, calling himself the Site Director, had banned the youth club. Darren did not know why, or for how long the ban would last, he thought it was something that a youth had done the previous week, but all he knew was that we were not to be let in. We got Basil's home phone number and rang him, standing as we were in the freezing night.

He said it was because some youths had interfered with the masks made by the Youth Theatre Group the previous week, and he had no choice but to ban us. We asked why he had said nothing to us at the time, and why had he not had the courtesy to inform us before we turned up. With much persuasion, he agreed to meet me the next day at two.

The next day at two I turned up to see him in his office. It was locked, but I could see him in there through the glass window. He did not respond to my knocking, so I went to get Darren. He went in, came out and said Basil was busy. I said I had an appointment, and when would he be free? The answer came that he did not want to see me at all. I asked Darren why this should be, as he had agreed to see me the night before. Darren shrugged and said, "He's frightened of you, Bill."

"Frightened of me? A pensioner? What's he playing at?"

But it was no good, Basil refused to discuss it, despite letters under his door, entreaties, but not threats.

I rang the Grogg Chairman and met him; we arranged a meeting, with Town Councillors, District Councillors, and a trustee, who was a member of the offended Youth Theatre. We also took Kate and Bob from the Youth Service. Of course, Basil was there, but he said nothing. He was probably still scared of me.

We got an agreement to reopen in the Green Room, with certain rules and provisos, which we could have agreed at the start if we had been asked to. The Chairman promised that we could have the Scout Hut when the Scouts vacated it, which was in about four months. We wrote all this down, as it was the first firm promise ever made by the Grogg trustees. I apologised to the woman for her spoiled masks, a cow and a pig, apparently, and she seemed placated. I asked that the door onto the stage be locked in future, so our naughty lads could not repeat the escapade.

So we were let back, with bad grace from the Site Director, Basil. Then started a series of petty annoyances to the fabric of the Grogg, because of the way that Basil had shut us out. He had made it plain he didn't want a youth club anywhere near the Grogg. The Caretaker was always friendly towards us, and talked to the miscreants, making things a good deal easier, and preventing damage when he was around. But they came at night and broke windows, and things were very strained between us and Basil. It was reported that some kids had started a fire against the wall late one night, and youth club kids got the blame, as always. I asked for evidence that it was them, but Basil's mind was firmly closed, and nothing we said or did would encourage him to do what the Grogg constitution said he had to do. It was only a matter of time before something happened that would mean our permanent exclusion, as it had years before. The Grogg had not changed, it only got a decent Chairman once in a while. Basil did what he wanted, it was obvious, and the current Chairman had no influence over him.

Connexions, once known as the Youth Employment Service, started a youth club down at the Pavilion on the Conway Fields. This was a much more suitable location, as there was a huge playing field with play equipment for little kids to use right outside the door. The actual rooms were very small, but it had a kitchen, a toilet, even though it was not built to be kid-proof. For a while there was no County Youth Club, but I helped the Connexions people. They were excellent, having run youth clubs before in other places. They knew a fair few of the youngsters too, from their school work. They were very welcoming to me, and we got on well from the start.

The trouble was in the building. It was used by adults during the day, and the plaster was easily marked, damage was hard to mend. We had a lot of kids in too, especially in the cold winter nights when they could not go outside and 'interact' in the dark and the cold. We had up to seventy members at a time, which meant almost non-stop policing. This is very tedious, and gets in the way of making proper relationships with the kids. It had to be done, or we would have been thrown out, as the Elcaster Opportunities

Committee who ran the building were already getting wary. You could not blame them, but I did try to keep the co-ordinator friendly to us. Her name was Shirley Racketts, she was a force of nature, and took no prisoners. If she liked you, you could do no wrong, if she didn't, you might as well be dead, she would do nothing for you. Luckily, she liked me, and we had many good laughs together, but she detested teenagers, didn't want them near the Pavilion. I talked her round many times, but she never changed her mind completely.

The County did not work with Connexions. I never found out why, but the reasons were political. Then the Education Service left the Infant School , and the buildings were vacated, and not used for anything. Bob negotiated with them to use them for a County Youth Club, and eventually got his way. We opened up at Moorfields, in a rather battered but large hut. Now Elcaster had two youth clubs in a week, and I went to both of them.

By this time I had finally retired from all teaching, for good, definitely, no returning. I received my fourth leaving present from St. Bens, having taken the decision when I was teaching the Naughty Boys on my 65th birthday. I had taken on this class at the request of the Science Department at St. Ben's, who were all women. The school had earlier done an experiment, splitting the boys from the girls just for science. This had worked well for the girls, but none of the women teachers wanted to teach the boys. So they asked me to come back, not telling me the precise reason, which was to take over the Naughty Boys. I was a little shocked when I discovered what the women had done, but it was too late to turn back.

At first, they were awful. Without girls, their sense of humour was that of a five-year-old. Farts were laughed at wildly, they did little homework, they just behaved like boys will at 14 with no girls around to civilise them. I worked as hard with them as I have ever worked with any class in school, and eventually it paid off, but very slowly. I threw out a couple of bad lads permanently, and the Head of Science took them over.

The women teachers said they smelled, and had to open windows after they had been in. I agreed, they smelled like Boys, which is what we smelled of when I was at school. One day, Ms. Tara, the Goth Head of Science, came into the room when I had gone to fetch something. I found them silent in front of her. They feared her sharp sarcasm, and listened.

"Oh, I'm so sorry, Ms. Tara. Were they making too much noise?"

"No, Mr. Bayley. I want to talk to them about Personal Hygiene." And she did. For five minutes she told them about deodorants, showering frequently, how sweat smells if not washed off. They listened in silence. "Remember what I have told you, lads. It's for your own good." And out she went.

Nobody spoke. It was no use going on with the Periodic

Table, so I asked them if they knew why farts smelled. They didn't know, so we discussed it for a while. Jenny the Lab assistant came in.

"Why did Ms. Tara come in? Were they talking too loudly, Bill?"

"No, Jenny, they were making a loud smell." We couldn't speak for laughing for a minute. The Naughty Boys did not see the joke.

Later that week, they asked the male P.E. teacher if they *did* smell. He told them they did, and to shower more often and use deodorants. From then on, my science classes were often conducted to the gentle hiss of an air-freshener, or the exchange of the latest masculine spray. Ms. Tara had done the trick all right, but they were no better behaved, for all that.

I thought as I wrote on the board on my 65th birthday, 'I am now getting my fourth pension, and I am officially an Old Age Pensioner, so what am I doing still here at the chalk face?' So I gave in my notice, with instructions that I really meant it this time; please, Deputy Head, do not ask me again, I may be tempted, but it would be Wrong. I am a pathetic addict, having to get my fix of teenagers weekly, but I really must get over it. Besides, I still have the Youth Club to meet them in.

FAREWELL TO THE NAUGHTY BOYS

So the time has finally come to part company. You go on your ways to the Future, I go mine into dusty retirement and preparation for death. Or vice versa, if we are all incredibly unlucky. I would like to review the past two years of our involvement with each other, as this is the end of an era for all of us, and a little reflection upon what our strivings have meant seems fitting.

We must draw a veil over some of the events. In fact, many veils. Now I come to think of it, a bloody great enormous curtain a mile wide wouldn't even get near to covering the strange yet weirdly comic happenings that have punctuated our struggle. So to hell with the veils.

I well recall the first time we set out to do an 'experiment' on speed. You were equipped with rulers and watches, and you wandered vaguely over St Benedict's fields in search of something moving. Or so you pretended. In reality, you saw an opportunity to doss and chat, whilst keeping me out of harm's way. One or two were deputed silently to engage me in earnest questions about the task, whilst the others got on with 'interacting', which involved teasing Ben and Simon, breaking rulers, chasing each other, and much more that I failed to see. I was not impressed by your zeal to learn physics. In this way, the struggle began. It went on for nearly two years

Your sense of humour soon made itself felt. Without girls in the class to raise their eyes to heaven in exasperation, you could indulge all your laddish jests with all the skills of hyperactive five-year-olds, and you did. All the time. The presence of girls might have raised the level a bit, improved the standard, but alas, they were absent. So we endured outbreaks of anal wind followed by fanning books, gasps and giggles. Needling each other when my back was turned became an art form. Denials of guilt were imperative, as were the ghastly false apologies after guilt was established. Guy, you were (no, are), appallingly good at this. I quite admire your trick of chewing, swallowing it when challenged, then denying guilt, which technically was by then correct. I just wish you hadn't done that 205 times, that's all.

I enjoyed the Russian roulette game of Sending You Out. If it was at the right time of the afternoon, there was the risk of The Headmaster coming along. I felt no guilt when some were executed on the spot, it was the luck of the draw, a useful lesson about the arbitrariness of Life. There were times when some of you were coming in and out like Autumn leaves, but neither of us ever stopped our behaviours. We couldn't, we were prisoners of reflex actions, trapped in a Dance of School Discipline.

There were more unusual events, like the time I got an anonymous note in Richard's minute writing, telling me he feared for his life because of danger from explosives. The "explosives" turned out to be used .303 cartridges brought in by one of the more warlike pupils, who shall remain nameless, Ben. No harm was done.

Naturally, one or two fell by the wayside, never to darken my classroom doors again, but at least one of them agreed that it was for the best. Others of you might have felt like going, but luckily for us both, you lacked the courage. Some of you, about four, I estimate, have never been sent out of my class. This is an experience that you will have to miss now, as it is too late; I'm sure your education will not suffer much though, Paul, Sam, Tom and Luke.

Finally, forgetting the Great Smell Controversy, what can we conclude? What was the point of our struggle? Did it do any good in the battle between Good and Evil? I think it did. I enjoyed your company, your jokes, your dogged resistance to learning. It is what boys are for.

Whether you will pass your Science exams or not, God alone knows. I have done what I thought was necessary, sometimes going a bit far over the top, as you did. But not so far over the top that we couldn't come back smiling, pretending it was all just a joke. I did threaten to walk out a few times, blaming you for making me come back and teach you, but I wouldn't really have done it. I think. Probably not, anyway.

But you are my swan song, my last drink before closing time, my final curtain. (I know Harry Lauder had 24 Final Last Tours, but this time I REALLY mean it). I would like to thank you from the bottom of my heart for being so normal, so archetypically schoolboys, such as have existed since the human race began. If the future of we old people is in your hands, then I have no fears, well, not many at any rate. Don't become doctors just yet, though. And don't send me out again, please Guy. And may we all experience the very best that life can offer, whatever Fate may bring. Let's hope it's at least a C Grade, which will be, like you are, good enough.

(They all got C Grades and above, except one, who was without doubt one of the laziest boys I ever met. I saw him the other day, and he told me he was a builder, but was

thinking of training as a Counsellor. He might be good at that)

I was missing teaching quite a lot, as I knew I would. I had lost my audience, my arena for my performance, and a youth club is no substitute, since they are not the captive audience that classes are, they can leave if they want to. I did seek to find out once if I could behave like a teacher in the youth club, and I discovered that I could, provided I had some activity to do with them. I used to take my video camera to the club, and spend an hour or so making a video with them. The technique was one I learned off a Family Therapist. You get one to volunteer, ask him/her who he/she is, and some other details, like 'are you married', 'do you have children', etc. Then I ask, "Is your wife/husband here?", and they pick one to be that character. In the end they all have parts, and a rough scenario to act in, and you start filming. All the dialogue is improvised, and they have to stay in character all the time. At the end we all watch the video. I used to stop it and ask why they did certain things.

The usual scenario was the one they all lived in. A mother, a father, a few children, the neighbours, a police person, a social worker (much detested by all), sometimes a dog, a teacher, and so on. The scene was almost always set in the home, with some of the kids in trouble with the police, the social worker was always a nuisance. Then there would be a row with the neighbours, caused by the kids. Father would try to settle things, get angry and go down to the pub, coming back drunk and making more serious trouble. Mother was always the peacemaker, whether played by a boy or a girl, trying to keep the family united, and father always went to the pub when he lost the argument. It must have been the story that most of the kids knew, and some of the discussions about it were fascinating. Later, when the club was run by the Youth Service, I had to stop making videos, since their rules said I had to get written permission from the parents of every kid who took part, and it was simply too much fuss for nothing.

We had a new team of County youth workers by now. Kate had left because her new job put too much pressure on her, and she didn't have the energy for a youth club. She had got promotion because of her involvement in youth work, as she had to deal with awkward customers, and her company thought that if she could deal with teenagers, she could deal with anything. I was really sorry to see her go, as she was fun to work with, serious about it, and put a lot of herself into her work. She had run a football tournament at which parents were invited, but none came. It didn't put Kate off, she had grit, a much-needed quality in youth work.

Our new senior worker was 'PT', a West Indian with a lot of urban experience, and who worked from Studley, not knowing Elcaster. Bob by this time was a Manager, and not liking it at all. He was supposed to manage Shirley Racketts, the co-ordinator of Elcaster Opportunities at the Pavilion, but you might as well try to manage a tornado. She was not kind to him, and there was bad feeling. This was a pity, as both of them were fine workers in their own fields, and should have been allowed to work separately, except for the idiocy of the 'management' concept, which had wrecked industry and was set to wreck everything else. People do not need managers; they can manage themselves. They might need co-ordinating, training, advising or smacking, but they do not need managing. It is childish and demeaning to both parties, and in a good organisation there are none, only supervisors.

We had two young women, Pat and Charlie, mostly untrained and inexperienced, but they were willing to learn, and got on with the kids, which is eighty percent of the job. Sometimes old professionals have lost the will to live, and drag themselves to the club, only to bore everyone including themselves, and squabble with the kids, then grumble about them. New people are never like that, and what they lack in experience they make up for in enthusiasm. It is always wonderful to see how pleased they are when the kids talk to them properly, usually after a few weeks, having been assessed by the youngsters and found to be OK. A middle-aged neighbour of mine, Sally, had asked me if she would enjoy youth work. I privately doubted it, but I told her to stick by me for a session, which she did. I was amazed when she said she had enjoyed it, and came back the next week. She got to be an excellent youth volunteer, and the kids used to tell her all sorts of things they never told me. She said to me once that she didn't like them swearing near her. "They don't swear AT me, Bill. I just don't like to hear it when they swear in their ordinary talk."

"Then tell them, Sally. They know you well enough by now. Tell them without getting cross. They'll do their best to curb it, I bet." And they did. Sally was surprised.

I got on well with all of them. After every session we had a debriefing session, where we talked about what had happened that night, and what we might do next week. Our leader PT seemed efficient and was liked by the kids. He organised a few trips in the Summer holidays, to drive go-carts, to Alton Towers, and other places of delight to the kids, but I was glad I didn't have to go. I was becoming everybody's grandfather, since the young workers were not much different in age to the kids in my eyes, but I would never have told them so.

The Scouts left their hut at the Grogg, and we asked Basil if he would honour his promise, made in front of all those official councillors. He muttered about it not being in a fit state to be used, so Bob found that he could get some official money to bring it up to scratch. Nothing happened, predictably. It has not happened to this day. So the only firm promise I ever got out of the Grogg trustees has never been honoured. And they wonder why nobody trusts them.

As there were now two youth clubs in the Town, you

might expect kids to use both, on separate nights of the week. Some did, but most of them preferred the one in the Pavilion. They said it was because it was nearer to their homes, which it was, but I think it was more subtle than that. The kids' Leaders went to the Connexions club. Leaders are always very hard to spot. Even the kids themselves were not conscious of who the leaders were, they just followed them, without knowing why. Adults are like that about pubs in the Town, it is a natural human trait. The one in the old infant school in Moorfields did look run down, and we had no money to improve it. The owners, the Education Authority, were not interested either, as it was destined to be knocked down and the land sold for building.

Things never go smoothly for long in the youth club trade, and there was some trouble over PT and his management of the people under him. I did not realise how disliked he was by the young women, and some of the older ones in Studley. For reasons I cannot now recall, I applied to become an employee of the County Youth Service, and allow PT to concentrate of Studley whilst I ran Elcaster with the two girls, Pat and Charlie, with Sally as a volunteer. I became the oldest new employee of Warwickshire Youth Service ever, and it had its downsides too. Now I was paid for the first time ever in my 30 years of youth work, I had rules I had to abide by. One of them was smoking, not only in the hut but on the premises. Poor Bob had to tell me I was not permitted to smoke my pipe anywhere in the grounds. I laughed at first, but Bob was serious; after all, he was a Manager. Then things went really pear-shaped. I will not go into what happened, as it was nasty and too recent, and nobody came out of it well. There was an official hearing about PT, and he was sacked. Then I fell out with one of the girls at the club, so I quit. After all, I was well over seventy, what was I doing still messing about in youth clubs?

I went on going to the Connexions club. They were unaffected by the row over PT, but things were not going well there either. Some of the older boys resented Dick, the young Connexions man, who told them off rather frequently, because he had to. They behaved badly on a couple of trips, and the women were becoming very cautious with them. There was damage to the walls inside, which we got away with paying for, but when one of them threw a bottle against the door frame, narrowly missing the glass, that was the last straw for the Committee, and they banned the club meeting in the Pavilion.

The Connexions looked at the hut we had used in Moorfields, but it had been broken into, and glass smashed on the floor. It looked even sadder that I had known it, and Connexions refused to work there, saying it was not safe. They were right, but it meant that the County club dribbled on there for a few more months, then ran out of members. They agreed with Connexions, it was not fit for use.

So from having two clubs the Town now had none. The County sent in two street workers, who met at the Pavilion, where a few kids would go to meet them and have a chat. Neither of the women were Elcaster people, so the kids were few in number. I went down a few times, but it was not a youth club by any means. I started a club of my own, called the One Henley Street Club, open on Mondays, for anyone to come in for a chat. No games, no running around, it was talk or nothing, with free tea and biscuits. The most I got was about twelve, but some nights there were none.

I met one of the lads at the Pavilion one night, and asked him if he was coming next week. For some reason, he was annoyed with me, and was rude. This is a transcript of our conversation, typical of how teenagers talk in their angry moments.

Dialogue, Pavilion, Alcester. 11th November 2010 6.30 p.m.
BB....Bill Bayley
M....Milky
A....Anita, street youth worker

M; I ent coming to your club no more, Bill.
BB: Please yourself. It's not compulsory.
M: I'll give you my membership card back.
BB: No need. You'll change your mind in three days anyway.
M: No I won't. I ent coming no more.
BB: OK, OK. I don't really care, Milky. Please yourself.
M: I don't want to come no more, Bill. I don't like it.
BB: All right. Don't come. Let's drop it, shall we?
M; I think you're a ******** *(muttered)*

A: Don't be rude, Milky.

M; I ent being rude. It's true. *(Goes to sit by Anita and farts loudly)*

A: You're just like an animal.

BB: And you're adding to global warming. Methane.

M: I don't care.

BB: You don't care about global warming? When the world burns up, I'll come looking for you.

M: You won't be able to do anything, 'cos we'll both be dead.

BB: In the long run, yes. But I shall catch you before I die.

M: What'll you do to me if you catch me, Bill?

BB: Oh I don't know. Nothing much.

M: Will you rape me?

BB: No. I am a man of wealth and taste. *(All except Milky laugh)*

M: What will you do if you catch me, though?

BB: Oh, drop it, Milky. I won't catch you. All right?

M: You just want to ********* *(mumbled)*

Boy in Cap :He's trying to do something for the community, Milky. You shouldn't say that.

M: Well, I'm not coming to your club anyway.

A: Can't you just drop it, Milky?

M: You just want to get ten boys in your place and rape them.

BB: If you say that again, I shall be forced to take action. Do you understand? Saying something like that is a criminal act. Slander. I could sue you , or your guardian, for that. Do you understand me, Milky? Saying that kind of thing in front of witnesses is criminal slander, and if you say it again I shall have to do something. Understand?

M: *(mumbles something)*

BB; Have we finished here? I'm leaving now. Milky, are you taking any drugs?

M: No

BB: Well, I'm going to have a word with your father about this. I take it very seriously.

M: I don't care.

(Exit Bill Bayley)

I have always been very aware of the power of malicious gossip, particularly anything about sex. Elcaster is like all small Towns, and big ones too, it runs on gossip. It is a measure of how we care for each other, but hearing bad things about people always has that extra spice, although we know it's wrong to do it. So I had to be angry at Milky, I could not afford to allow what he said in temper to spread around, and I fully intended to talk to his Dad. For some reason, I let it rest that night.

The next night Milky tapped on my front door. I asked him in, sat him down and let him talk.

"I'm sorry I said what I said last night, Bill."

"That's alright. Is that why you've come, to say sorry?"

"Yes. I shouldn't have done it."

"Did your Dad tell you to come?"

"No. I told him, and he said to keep out of your way for a bit."

"Did anyone else tell you? Anita, for instance?"

"No, no-one told me . I just came."

"Why did you come, then, Milky?"

"I had a bad conscience about it. I knew it was wrong."

"Why was your conscience bad?"

"Because you told my Dad that I was a good kid a few months back."

"Well, you are. And having the courage to face me after I had been so angry with you made me think you are an even better kid than I thought. Let's say no more, then, I will not say anything to your Dad, if you don't want."

We shook hands, as men do, and he went home.

So there is no youth club in Elcaster now. Except that last year I was asked if a fund-raising committee could use the name of the EYP to apply for a grant to build a youth club.

"Why the EYP? You haven't a hope, anyway. Youth clubs are old hat."

"We want to use your organisation because you fit the requirements. You have a Bank Account, a Committee, a Constitution, and you have been going nearly twenty years. And maybe we haven't a hope, but it's worth a try, you must admit, Bill."

So they tried, and got £175.000 to build a new youth club. I was gobsmacked. The EYP was two of us, and we had to be reconstructed to cope with all this money. They made me stay as Chairman. The building has been started, and just as I was thinking to sit back and watch the County run the New Youth Club, the news came that the County were disbanding their Youth Service.

Thanks! Now we shall have to get volunteers together and run it like it used to run. At least there won't be Rules and Regulations in bucketfuls, we won't even have to get Criminal Record Bureau checks, as long as we know each other. Bob may lose his job, of course, but he is wanting to get the new club together with me.

There's no fool like an old fool, goes the saying. I didn't think Old Age would be like this. I hadn't planned to run a youth club. At the age of seventy four I am going to put together the people to run a teenagers' youth club for one night a week.

Why? If you have read as far as this, perhaps you can tell me. I would love to know.

STEP ELEVEN -- THE END BIT, THE ONLY HARD STEP

A POEM FOR 2025, written in 1994

Yes, I knew Richard , many years ago
When I taught a bit of art at Benny's

(That was what we called Saint Benedict's, you know)
But where was I? I'm nearly ninety now
And memory isn't what it used to be.
Oh, yes, the lad called Jones. I didn't think
He'd get so far, he seemed a pleasant boy,
But like them all in Benny's, they didn't do much work,
An idle lot, but harmless, not a wicked one there.
No, I couldn't foresee what he would do,
There was no means of telling what anyone would do
In those days, it's not like now, you clever folks
Predict the twists and turns of life before it's lived.
I don't approve at all, I think it's wrong,
But you don't care what an old man like me thinks,
Do you? I can see you don't, and there's no need to hide your smile.
But I still think that what he did
Was beyond guessing, even now. Who'd have thought
Just what was in that fifteen-year-old head?
He seemed a nice enough lad, as I have said,
But to do all that ---- well, I wish I'd got his autograph
Then, in 1994, when he was young. It would be worth a fortune now
I dare say. What did he look like?
You TV people always ask those kinds of things,
As if it matters. He was in Year 10, a boy, with friends,
I dare say; his hair was short, I think, and he made a lot of jokes
Not all of them were funny, but he thought they were.
Did I teach him anything? I doubt it,

Not many listened to teachers then, it's not like now,
But I don't think he remembers me at all.
Why should he? He had his life ahead of him,
And everything was wonderful, the future, up in front,
He seemed to have no worries, he was like the rest,
An individual, careless, sometimes a little pest,
But nothing that would make you stop and think
"That boy wants watching". No, I probably did not
Give him ideas that could have led him
After all these years to be the man
He has become.

Who would have thought it? Yes, I knew him,
That Richard Jones.

Youth clubs will last as long as England has a Class System, which is probably for ever. As we are world-class hypocrites, we barely even acknowledge that we have a Class System. It is not such a bad thing to have one, places like India, China, USA, all have a Class Systems, and they all operate with different rules, mostly secret ones. India even has a caste system on top, but the Indians can cope with a seriously multilayered society without any trouble; it has done it for 10.000 years.

Youth clubs are a product of the class war in England.

Perhaps the word 'war' is a bit strong now that the Trades Unions have lost their power temporarily, but the conflict between the classes is a continuous process, one in which at present, the year 2011, the Lower Classes are losing to the Upper Classes. It will not always be so, the battle will begin again in earnest any day soon.

The definition of the Classes changes all the time. At one time society seemed to know which class was which; the Upper Class was the Aristocracy and the Old Rich, with the New Rich panting at their heels. The Lower Class was anyone who laboured and got paid. Many thought of themselves as Middle Class, but that was, and still is, a cop-out. There is no Middle Class, any more than there are people who are Middle Sex. We are either Men or Women. We are born that way, unlike the Class system, where mobility is possible, if slow.

Youth clubs are the organisations for the unorganisable, clubs for the unclubbable. This will always be so, as there are always people like that. But they are spread evenly through the classes, yet youth clubs are exclusively for the lowest in society, or so people think, and at present they are not far off the truth. It need not always be so. I look forward to the time that the sons and daughters of the Upper Class (ie the Rich nowadays) who are rebellious, stupid, uncivilised and in need of discipline will come to youth clubs for some part of their education. As things are, the Public Schools cater for these people now, and there are very many rebellious, stupid, and uncivilised kids who have private education, to the detriment of the schools concerned.

The division of England into two classes dates right back to before Roman Times. Note that I say 'before Roman Times', not 'Ancient British Times', nor even 'Celtish Times.' The Upper Class wrote our history, and they regarded Celts as Lower Class, since they couldn't write. It wasn't so much that they couldn't, it was just that they didn't. Anyway, the history writers dismiss them, and to them, history begins with the Romans, who could write, and had O Level Latin, at least. They could all have gone to Oxbridge, if it had been invented then. But once the Romans were here, all the Celts became Lower Class, and doubtless started to Act Up, stage strikes, fight on the streets, smash windows when drunk, and generally set the tone for 2000 more years of class warfare. You can see it to this day on the High Street of Elcaster on a Friday, a fine old tradition that is still maintained, despite the efforts of the Romans (sorry, 'the police') and the moans of the aspiring Middle Classes.

I have been unable to find out from the experts whether the Celts had youth clubs or not. If they did have, they were probably run by the Romans, and might have had the same aims as I did, to talk to the natives and find out what they thought, and how they worked. This would lead to greater integration of the Classes, and the brighter of the Celts could in the fullness of time become honorary Roman Citizens. The Romans were very keen on this, as it promoted stability and peace throughout the Empire. I have always had the same aim, for the same reasons. I would rather be governed by civilised ex-youth club members than any number of Public School toffs or simpering Middle Class liberals. They would know a lot about how their society actually works, since they would have been right through it. As far as I know, there are no ex-youth club members from Elcaster in the cabinet, or at least they are not admitting it. I have high hopes, though.

I love this country, with its past power and its convoluted history. We never like to throw anything away, which is why the French call us hypocrites. They don't understand that we can face two ways at once, one way because it was how we used to do it, and the other way because that is new and modern. We executed our King a century before the French got round to it, and then we called his son back, but under different rules. Social Evolution is what we do, not Revolution, which always dumps you back where you started, as the French and the Russians should know, but don't. We shall never change the fact that we have Rich and Poor. Even Jesus said, "The poor are always with us." It is inevitable that people should have different levels of wealth, just as we have different levels of intelligence, diligence, honesty, whatever you care to name.

At the present moment, 2011, a youth underclass has been created, who have no useful qualifications, no jobs, no visible future in work, and are not valued by the ruling classes. This cannot continue without repercussions. Most of the youth club members I know belong to this underclass. This was not true until about fifteen years ago, when education and the world of work conspired to shut the door of aspiration for these kids, and things only get worse. Nothing is being done, the problem is invisible to the government and employers. It is not invisible to parents and members of what used to be called the Working Class, though.

When a few months ago I had twelve lads in to my One Henley Street Club. Eleven had no jobs, no prospects, and little hope for the future. They were all living at home and paying no rent to their parents. Only one was not living at home, he was living in a tiny hotel room paid for by Social Services,with no cooking facilities, and no meals provided. His foster-parents had thrown him out. He too had no job, though he was desperately trying to find one. Three months later, he still has not found one.

But what I am sad about is how badly the Rich behave. Surely they have enough just to be richer than us. Why must they have everything better? Education, life-span, access to pretty women, they snatch everything in such a greedy way. At one time the rich had a conscience, and donated Good Works to the Poor. Even in the Fifties, David Grogg gave more than £50,000 to build the Grogg Hall in memory of his dead wife. What do the rich do like that now? They clutch their cash to their chests and hope we don't notice how greedy they are. Or if they are Bankers, they just don't care what we think, they brazenly flaunt their bonuses. Better not overdo it, you rich. The poor may feel they have nothing to lose in the future, and they will take it away from you, like in a Revolution. It has never happened here yet, but if the gap widens between the haves and the Have Nots, who can say?

Which brings me back to the kids who go to youth clubs. They have had the rough end of the education stick, with large class numbers, and courses that are meaningless to them. Why have we never got round to educating them properly, with stuff they can use to earn money, start businesses, and so on. The Education Establishment thinks they are hopeless, and money should not be wasted on their education, and they just take it, without complaining enough. The authorities use the 'fact' that their behaviour shows how ignorant they are. The reverse is true; they behave badly because they think they are being ignored and despised. They are right. It is the duty of the wealthy to educate the poor, because they have the money and the means to do it. Unless they do it, and do it well, the whole country becomes an unpleasant place to live in, and there is always a risk of revolution if it becomes extreme. But the rich are not clever enough to see this, they are scared of the poor because they don't know them, and you are always frightened of the Unknown.

Things are not very bad in this Town, of course. The balance between the classes oscillates all the time, but it is one of the functions of politics to ensure the balance is restored when it goes off-centre. The trouble is, so much energy is put into restoring the balance that no progress is made. Perhaps it is not 'progress' I mean, but just the endless tug-of-war that goes on, and the only 'progress' we make is to get wealthier and use more and more technology.

As a society, we seem to be getting more divided, less social, more composed of individuals. I think this dates from the infamous statement by Margaret Thatcher, 'There is no such thing as society'. She didn't invent that attitude, it was already in the air, in the USA especially. It had led to a culture of Celebs, famous merely for being famous, lacking in skills of any kind save that of getting noticed, and remaining in the media eye by any means. Skills are being abandoned in the Admired Classes, it's smart to be unsmart, it's not what you know, it's who you know. It's becoming dog eat dog, a War of All Against All, as the philosopher Hume said. Socialism is retreating all over the globe, being replaced by a capitalism that recognises only individual worth, and has only a vague understanding of how wealth is actually created. It doesn't care much how it is done, only what the results are, measurable profit.

I find all this profoundly sad. It is the opposite of how I was brought up, how my country was run, and what I believe. I am unable to do anything much about it, though. The only thing I can do is to do the opposite wherever I find myself. I long ago abandoned Socialism as a governing force, as it is too vulnerable to sharks and predatory people to work on a large scale. So I decided that it was not worth voting Socialist, and then along came Tony Blair with New Labour, a most unsocialist party with mainly Mrs. Thatchers principles. If I am to call myself a socialist, then I have to act as one when I am doing anything. (That is the pity about Christianity. If only Christians would act as Jesus told them, the world would be a lot better, but they do nothing of the kind). On the other hand, maybe I'm wrong about the way the world is going. I probably take too much notice of the media, who sell themselves by peddling disasters. I care about it, though, but I don't have to join in now I'm retired, and living in a backwater. My kids and grandchildren have to live in it, and they must make of it what they will.

I want to help to make a better, fairer, society. That has always been behind my reasons for teaching and for running youth clubs. I try to include everyone, not as an equal, but with equal consideration. This is not hard to do on the tiny scale that I work on, it is much more difficult on a big scale, but if enough people would do it, the place might slowly change. Whether it will or not is not something that I worry about any more. I must be responsible for myself and my actions, and try to influence others to do it too. But if I fail, it is not my fault; I have done my best, and that has to be good enough. I would make myself miserable thinking about how things are not going as I would like them to, if I thought it was in any way my responsibility. All I can do is to act, and speak about what I do, here and in my paper, The Bear Flag. I am driven to do that, not in a compulsive way, but because that is the nature of my soul now. If I have a soul, that is.

Maybe I have come to some conclusion about why I am still running youth clubs by writing this book. It dates back to my own teenage, when I was a public-school boarder. If you stepped out of line, you got the cane. Or you were expelled, and I did not like the cane, nor want to be expelled. So I behaved myself. I was even good at being a Public-school Boy, until I got fed up with it. But I never rebelled.

Maybe my brain never reorganised itself, like they know now that a teenager's brain does. It is possible that it only got round to reorganisation when I went to help in my first youth club, and my brain recognised what it had missed. It started on the process, and it still hasn't finished. So by my own definition, I am a bit mad, and still a teenager at heart, and in mind. That is the nearest to an explanation of my wanting to run youth clubs, which has puzzled me now for years.

Now I read that back to myself, it doesn't really hold water. So the mystery remains, like all good mysteries, my own private Loch Ness Monster.

YOUTH CLUBS: YOUR QUESTIONS ANSWERED.

<u>How do I set about starting a youth club?</u> Find some youths

and ask them if they want a club. Then find a place to set it up. This last step may take some time, and you may get downhearted, especially if the youths you have asked start to shout at you in the street, and mock you for being a wimp and making promises you cannot keep. If you are destined to run a youth club, carry on. If not, pack up now and take up macramé.

I want to start a youth club, but I do not always like youngsters. What should I do? Nothing. Nobody can like youngsters all the time, even they themselves. At times I have detested them. But if you have to ask that question before you start, then don't start. Find a group of people who you will like all the time. When you do, you will find you have died and gone to Heaven. Grow up.

How do you control behaviour without using violence? Never use violence of any kind, even verbal violence, in public. It starts the others off, sets a bad example, and it is illegal; you will find yourself in court in the wink of a teenagers eye. They know the Law. However, threatened violence in private works wonders. Here is how to do it:

Take the offender aside, make sure nobody is listening, and ask them if they recall Tom breaking a leg, or some young person who suffered drastic injury recently. When they say yes, you say 'That was me did that.' When they express scorn, say 'I haven't always been a nice youth leader, you know. You don't know what I did before I came here. I have met some seriously bad men in my time, some when I was in prison/ the army/ mental hospital. Look, I don't want to have to do this, but they don't like me being disrespected. I only have to say the word, and they come down from Leicester and do whatever I ask, They owe me, see. They actually love their work. Now, you aren't going to do that again, are you? Good lad/lass!' You must say all this, with variations if necessary, with an absolutely straight face. I have never known it fail, but it must not be overused. Of course, if you really do know violent lads from Leicester, what are you asking me stupid questions for, then?

What do you do about drugs? You can't afford to allow them in the club, but never be righteous and holier-than-thou about the subject. All of them will have tried cannabis, in the form of Skunk-weed. By all means tell them about the connection between skunk and schizophrenia, and tell them what the symptoms of psychosis are (if you don't know, look it up on Google). Some will tell you they already hear voices, or see visions; don't necessarily take any action about it, but watch for other signs of madness. This is difficult, because being a teenager IS a form of madness, which they get over in time. The ones that don't get over it go to prison, mental hospital, or into politics. Or become teachers, or, worse, youth club workers. If you hear they are trying the stronger drugs repeatedly, report them to the authorities, but first the parents. I have no compunction about this, I tell them that is what I do, so they never tell me if they are doing hard drugs. That is the way I want it. If they do tell you, it is a cry for help, above your pay grade, so report them, since they lack the courage to turn themselves in. They want addiction treatment, which you cannot begin to provide.

What if some of the teenagers show symptoms of mental

illness? Get this straight, they all show symptoms of mental disturbance, much of the time. That is because they ARE mentally disturbed, as you were at their age. There is a huge amount of evidence coming from brain imaging, a new research tool, that human brains undergo a colossal reorganisation between the ages of 13 and 19, which we call puberty. This is not just sex hormones coursing through the body, it is the emergence of self-awareness, amongst a lot of other changes in consciousness. They are having to cope with this, as well as parents, pressure at school, pressure from their peers, pressure from the media to be 'normal teenagers' (as if there were any such animal!), and the acute sense of loss that comes with leaving innocent childhood behind for ever. Don't think that just because someone behaves like a yob that they don't have fine sensibilities. It may be that is the reason for their behaviour. It may also be that they are a born yob. Certainly, you cannot tell which they are when they are young, so give them the benefit of the doubt, give them some space to act mad, bad and sad. They may not get another chance. And you yourself may find you need to do that with them, too. A youth club is a fine place for grown-ups to act very silly indeed, since no-one will notice, you are just like the rest.

Shouldn't we forget about youth clubs, and move on to a Modern way of dealing with youngsters? Can you suggest what would take their place? Are you a politician, or a Tory voter seeking to save money? What's wrong with them? What's wrong with you? You might like to come down and see what we do, talk to some of them. Can I recruit you as a potential volunteer? Perhaps you might like to get to know them before your kind force them to take from you what is rightfully theirs. It might save your life one day. It will make you into a bigger human being, that's certain.

<u>What would Jesus say about youth clubs?</u> I think He might just want to run one. He would be very welcome in ours, and a few miracles would go down well with the kids. He was concerned with the publicans and sinners, after all. It is true that hardly any teenagers appear in the New Testament, but there must have been some around. Unless people were born adults then. Jesus himself was a baby, and went into the synagogue at the age of ten to ask the Rabbis questions. Perhaps one of them was "When will you run a youth club for us?" He wouldn't care for the bad behaviour, but inside the club there isn't much, and I don't care for it either. Turning the other cheek is what you really learn how to do when you work in a youth club. It's not being a wimp, either, it's treating unpleasantness with pleasantness and firmness. Come down and try it, be a volunteer, and practice Christianity as Jesus told it. It's really hard, but you can get there if you want to.

<u>What is the Purpose of Youth Clubs?</u> I have thought long and hard about this question, for all of my 33 years involvement. I have decided that they have no purpose at all. They merely exist, like the Poor, or wasps. They don't need a purpose, although many people think they do. When I was young and green, I spoke to the Town Council about why I wanted to run a youth club. I said it was 'to keep kids off the streets." Len Wade, then an Elcaster councillor, who came

here from London, stood up and said, “What's wrong with the streets, Mr. Bayley? I did most of my courting on the streets.” He was right. There is nothing wrong with the streets, it's what some people do on them that can be wrong. It's the same with youth clubs, or any human institution. It's the people who make it, good or bad. So youth clubs have no purpose but to be a collection of people who interact with each other, mainly of young people, but with some tolerant adults too, and make the Universe a more joyful place.

You have been very patient. If you really want to run a youth club, this is what you do:
First, find a place. Imagine something like a pub for teenagers, with no alcohol. It should be welcoming, comfortable and safe. It should be free to go in. Your customers will ensure that it contains few people they do not like. They will need adults to keep a benevolent eye on them, but these adults should not interfere except to keep the peace from time to time. Would you want the barman in your pub telling you off constantly?
Second, just sit back and enjoy the atmosphere. Stop worrying. If activities are needed, someone will do them when they get bored. Do you want to be organised into activities in your pub all the time?

But enough of these questions. There is no use trying to write down how to do it. You might as well write down “How to be Good”. Or “Run a Youth Club in Ten Easy Steps”, and expect the text to inform people how to do it.

Forget it. You get the guidelines, and then you have to do it. Like a map guides you on a walk, but the magnificence of the actual landscape is not set down on the surface of the map. How could it be? This book is not even a map. The directions it seems to give are flawed. It is certainly not a history, but it is my history as I remember it in the twilight of my old age. Yet I am intending to run another youth club. Perhaps twilight has not arrived just yet.

THE END